GOOD LITURGY

SMALL PARISHES

Linda Osborn

Liturgy Training Publications

ACKNOWLEDGMENTS

Books don't just happen, especially first ones.
It helps to have encouragement from people
whose opinions influence you. This book
owes its existence to more people than I can
name, some of whom played a larger role
than others. Two of these are Kim Piron,
project coordinator for the San Bernardino
diocesan liturgical formation program, who
encouraged me to write, and Bob Piercy of
Liturgy Training Publications, who
encouraged me to submit the manuscript for
publication. A very special thanks to Gabe
Huck, director of Liturgy Training
Publications. It was his book on the Triduum
that first ignited my passion for liturgy and
other books of his that helped educate me in
this area. Among the people who read the
manuscript and made suggestions are Dr.
James Dallen and Marian Beaumier of
Gonzaga University in Spokane, Wash.; Carol
Trees and Mike Humphries in the San
Bernardino diocese, Calif.; and Mary Beth
Kunde-Anderson at the Chicago archdiocesan
Office for Divine Worship. Their time and
input was most helpful. Last but not least is
my editor, Martin Connell. His patience and
technical expertise have been invaluable, and
his friendly encouragement helped turn a
labor of love into reality. To these people and
to my parish family at St. Anne's in the
Mountains, heartfelt thanks. God bless each
of you.

Editor: Martin F. Connell
Production editor: Deborah Bogaert
Designer: M. Urgo
Art: Chuck Ludeke
Typesetter: Karen Mitchell
This book was typeset in Weidemann and
printed by Original Smith Printing.
Copyright © 1996, Archdiocese of Chicago:
Liturgy Training Publications, 1800 North
Hermitage Avenue, Chicago IL 60622-1101;
1-800-933-1800, FAX 1-800-933-7094. All
rights reserved.

Library of Congress Cataloging-in-Publication
Data
Osborn, Linda.
    Good liturgy, small parishes / Linda Osborn.
      p.   cm.
    1. Catholic Church — Liturgy.   2. Catholic
Church — United States — Liturgy.   I. Title.
BX1970.O69   1996
264' .02 — DC20   96-19271
                                            CIP

ISBN 1-56854-150-3
GDLIT

CONTENTS

For Steve

Your love and support
made this dream possible.

The beauty of Catholic liturgy has always touched me deeply, connecting me with the mysteries of God and with my brothers and sisters in the Body of Christ. Good liturgy can deepen our relationships with our God and with each other. Since Vatican II, workshops and books on liturgical practices have been abundant. They cover every aspect of liturgy, from building a better choir to improving your RCIA program and from forming liturgy committees to attending to art and environment beyond banners. These are all excellent resources. But what if your choir consists of only four or five people on a good day and your RCIA program has one candidate? What if your liturgy committee is you and your pastor? In other words, what if you are part of a small parish?

This has been my experience for the past nine years, and it is this experience that led me to think that a book especially for small parishes might be helpful. Perhaps the growing pains, the joys and frustrations, and the learning experiences of these past years could help someone else in their quest for good liturgy.

It was not my intention to become a liturgist when my husband, Steve, and I moved to a small mountain resort community. We moved there from a large suburban parish where we had been quite active in choir and in various other liturgical ministries. Expecting the same level of celebration in our new parish, we were unprepared for what we experienced. It was quickly apparent that there was no director of liturgy, nor even much direction to the liturgical celebration. A change of parish didn't change our situation; so we found ourselves increasingly involved in the various areas of liturgical ministry. Somewhere in this process, I found myself director of liturgy for a small parish in a mountain ski resort area.

INTRODUCTION

My first attempts were less than successful, due largely to a lack of knowledge — these past years have been on-the-job training. I will be forever grateful to the parish community of St. Anne's in the Mountains in Running Springs, California, for their patience and support during this learning process. Together we discovered the joy of celebrating well and have developed a liturgical life for our parish that belies our small numbers.

In the area of education, I had to rely on diocesan workshops and the conferences of larger organizations because there was no university nearby. These workshops and classes were accompanied by a great deal of reading. Currently, I have relocated and have returned to college to finish my degree in Religious Studies. By intention or not, a liturgist is what I have become, so my goal now is to continue learning and growing and to pass along what I have learned from my experiences in the hope that it may hasten the learning process for others.

Being part of a small parish is a wonderful opportunity to truly be community. Because the parish family is small in numbers, we know one another and share each other's joys and sorrows. While larger parishes struggle with forming small faith communities within their structures, we are already a small faith community. Seventy to eighty families makes for a close-knit parish family.

This same experience also led me to the conclusion that those of us who labor in small vineyards need some assistance. Virtually all workshops, seminars, conferences, books and guides assume at least a moderately large parish. True, the same liturgical principles apply regardless of the size of the parish; but the practicalities are quite different. With a little adaptation, the priceless treasures of our Catholic liturgies are just waiting for our small parish families.

My personal philosophy on the role of liturgy in parish life is summed up in Vatican II's *Constitution on the Sacred Liturgy:* "The liturgy is the summit toward which the activity of the church is directed; it is the fount from which all her power flows." To this end, in my opinion, it is vital that those parish ministers responsible for rites and rituals in the parish be well-trained and well-grounded, not only in basic theology and church history but specifically in those documents which give us the basic rubrics and ritual forms. It is important not simply to *know* the ritual but to *understand* its history, its symbolism and its role in today's church. We must know where we have been in order to see where we are going. It is also important to understand the roles of music and art in liturgy as well as the roles of each ministry within its structure — and to encourage them.

Once the basics — the ideals — are understood, it is crucial to have a pastoral concept of the parish. Because the Mass is the only opportunity for some people, and the major opportunity for most, to hear the word of God and be united with the mystical Body of Christ, these liturgies must invite, support and encourage the people of the community, assisting them ever further on their faith journey and bringing us all into closer union with God. "Every liturgical celebration is a sacred action surpassing all others. No other action of the church can equal its efficacy by the same title and to the same degree" (CSL, #7).

To this end, parish liturgists must be responsive to the needs of the people of their parishes. The celebration appropriate to an urban parish of 2000 families may not be appropriate to a rural parish of 200 families, even though both parishes follow the same rubrics of the *General Instruction of the Roman Missal.* Because one of the prime directives of *The Constitution on the Sacred Liturgy* is "full and active participation by all the people" (#14), liturgies must reach out to people and must be planned to assist in that full and active participation. While the rubrics need to be understood and followed, it is also important that the focus on those rubrics not be at the expense of the meaning and spirit behind them.

If parish liturgies are truly to be the fount from which all else flows, they must prepare, invite and support the ongoing conversion of the members of the community. Those liturgies must celebrate the unique ways in which each parish (1) helps people belong to and build up the Body of Christ, (2) engages them in a personal, communal struggle of conversion and reconciliation in Christ, and (3) works at re-creating the face of the earth in its community and beyond. Each parish liturgy must invite the faithful, focus their prayer, feed and unite their spirits and then send them renewed back into their everyday lives, able to live the gospel message to a needy world.

Most of what follows has been gleaned from other sources. There is nothing new or revolutionary in this book, only ideas on adapting rites, rituals and liturgical components. It contains suggestions on downsizing without compromising the basic principles and theology of liturgy. The ideas and thoughts presented here certainly aren't the last word but are rather observations and experiences that might help other liturgists see the possibilities as they assist their parishes in reaching a fuller, richer liturgical life in spite of, or even because of, their small size. This guide is meant to be a starting point.

If the tone of this book seems to imply that the reader is completely inexperienced or unknowledgable, that is not the intent. In order to cover as much as possible for as many as possible, some areas are quite basic. So if you are already working in the field of liturgy and have started the educational process, some of this information may seem redundant. But perhaps you will find it presented from a different point of view, thereby giving you a fresh approach. I always find it helpful to go back to basics from time to time, since later knowledge frequently influences the way old ideas are perceived.

Perhaps some of you have become involved with liturgy in your small parish after moving from a large urban parish. There are many of us "refugees from the cities" looking for a slower pace of life. We bring with us the expectations of liturgy as we experienced it in our larger parishes but may find a parish community that looks much as it did 25 years ago. Many people are definitely not experiencing the full and active participation of the assembly envisioned in the *Constitution on the Sacred Liturgy.* This doesn't mean that they have less devotion or faith; more than likely, there just hasn't been anyone willing to take on the task of liturgy planning or the burden of education and time that goes with the job. A pastor can only do so much. Also, many of these parishes do not see anything wrong with minimal liturgies and thus see no need for change or improvement.

This is not to say that mediocre liturgy is the sole domain of the small parish. In our travels, my husband and I have encountered some pretty pathetic liturgies in some very large parishes. Just because it is a cathedral does not guarantee it has fulfilling liturgy! We have attended liturgies in cathedrals that seemed concerned only with doing the minimum necessary in as short a time as possible. We have also been in communities of all sizes where Mass went on in the sanctuary while the assembly was engaged in their private prayers. No one spoke to, sang with or touched anyone else.

We have experienced the universality of our church and communities of faith in parishes of all sizes and in places as diverse as New York City, the Yucatán in Mexico, Montserrat in Spain and Grand Canyon National Park. A parish in Bend, Oregon, will always be a treasured memory of feeling welcome and being part of a fully active and participating community. The joy of their celebration was contagious. Likewise, a small parish in Cozumel, Mexico, surrounded us with warmth and welcome at their Saturday vigil Mass. The language barrier was no match for the bond of the Body of Christ.

Size alone neither causes nor corrects liturgical problems. It is a function of people, and only the People of God, working in harmony with the Holy Spirit, can make a difference. May the Holy Spirit guide you as you consider what is offered here and as you persevere in your ministry giving praise and glory to our God.

Chapter One

The Font from which All Flows

The People of God

Our celebration begins in the dark. We are gathered as a family on this particular night. The new fire leaps to the sky, rending the darkness. This fire is passed to a large candle and then to the small candles held by each person. By candlelight, our reason for being is sung and our story is told. "In the beginning. . . ." And thus our vigil is begun. Our story is told by many, accompanied by music and symbols as we move from the darkness of nothingness to our creation and formation as people of light, people of God. The Gloria rings out, the gospel is proclaimed. Once again we are an Alleluia people.

New members seeking to join our family are among us, waiting expectantly. We welcome them, reminding them — and ourselves — of what it is that sets us apart. We immerse them in the waters of death and life, clothe them in white and anoint them. And after they are washed, clothed and oiled, we lead them to the table of salvation and share in the eucharistic banquet.

We are completing our holy days of watching and waiting, which began with pomp and procession on Thursday as we washed feet, remembered our role as servants, commemorated the gift of our Lord as our very food and watched and waited with him at Gethsemani. On Friday we remembered his passion, adored his cross and waited. Now we joyously proclaim the resurrection with music and singing, with joy and ceremony, and with food and drink as we welcome each other and our new members into fellowship. We have brought the best of who we are and what we have to these days of celebration.

This could have been the scene in any cathedral or suburban parish in the country, with hundreds or thousands of people, but this Triduum celebration was in a small mountain parish of 75 families with no more than 125 people present. We had a choir, full processions and the participation of a large percentage of our community. Entire families were involved. Mom was preparing food for the reception while the kids cleaned the pews. A Boy Scout and his father volunteered to build the fire. One seven-year-old boy proudly read his part as Isaac in the second reading at the Vigil and found out that he too had gifts to offer. Not to be left out, his four-year-old brother wanted a part. He helped light the paschal candle from the fire. For these two children — and through them all who celebrated — the Vigil became part of our church's history.

The fullness of our common rites and rituals is not dependent on numbers but on God's grace and our desire and willingness to go the extra distance. Good liturgy doesn't just happen, whether in a large church or a small church. It requires effort.

The treasures of good liturgy beckon. Good liturgy is the best form of evangelization. It not only nourishes us but also strengthens us to the task of bringing the gospel message into our homes, schools and workplaces. By our words and deeds, nurtured in our liturgical celebrations, others come to know Christ. Our celebrations remind us of who we are and what we are called to be.

In our traditions we really do have a liturgical treasure. It is a 2,000-year-old treasure made even more sacred with the history of those who have gone before us. They have kept our story — our identity — alive and have passed it down to us in our liturgy. And liturgy done well shows off that treasure just as fine china and silver show off a culinary delight. In a small parish, we just set the table for fewer people.

What Is Our History?

Before we define the small parish, let's look at our history in general. How has God been revealed within the framework of small numbers? From the earliest traditions in Hebrew scripture, small groups of people and small communities have received God's attention and blessings. Starting in the Book of Genesis, where Abraham argues with God about how many righteous people must be found in Sodom to prevent the destruction of the whole city, the tradition highlights that with our God, small numbers make a difference. God would spare the city if only ten were found (Genesis 18:22 – 33). Later, in the seventh chapter of Deuteronomy, the people are told that God didn't choose them because of their large numbers. Indeed, they were "fewest of all peoples." That theme is reiterated in Psalm 105, in which it is sung that even when Israel was "few in number and of little account" God wouldn't allow anyone to oppress them.

When Jesus was teaching and healing, it was often within the context of small groups. His immediate group of followers was not large — the twelve apostles and several others — and certainly did not number in the hundreds. While he preached to the multitudes, he healed and taught in family groups, illustrated by the healing of Peter's mother-in-law (Luke 4:38) and the raising of the child of the synagogue leader (Mark 5:35 – 43). One conclusion that can be drawn from these and other examples is that a small group of people was as likely to receive the Lord's attention as a large group.

The synoptic gospels frequently link the mission of both Jesus and his disciples to houses and homes. In his study of house churches in Paul's time, Vincent Branick cites several instances of Jesus teaching at homes as well as acting as host or being a guest in a home. Branick suggests that this linking may "reflect the historical memories about Jesus and his first disciples." He further suggests that the stress on this linking of homes and mission reflects "a similar link in the communities producing these gospels."[1]

The witness to small churches in the New Testament letters is also strong. Most of it appears in Paul's letters addressed to local churches — for example, see the two references to Aquila and Prisca and their house church in his first letter to Corinth and again in his

Letter to the Romans. Paul's Letter to Philemon, only 25 verses in length, greets Philemon and those who meet in his house. In Colossians we find greetings to Nympha and her house church. From these references and others it appears that small assemblies of believers were not uncommon.

Some of our knowledge comes from other early church writers who have left us with descriptions of this emerging church gathering in individual homes to hear the word, to listen to the teachings of Jesus as related by the apostles and to celebrate the eucharistic meal in common. Most of these descriptions pertain to liturgical practices but are mentioned here because of their relationship to small house churches. In many ways, today's small parish or faith community is a reflection of these early communities.

Another, more modern historical matter that bears directly on the character of today's small parishes deals with the history of the Catholic church in the Americas. Catholics were the first non-native peoples in this country; they arrived through Spanish and French exploration and colonization. The southern portion of today's United States from California to Florida was first settled by the Spanish, who established Catholic missions. The French, who explored the Mississippi River area known as the Louisiana Territory, were also Catholics who brought their faith to this region. But later, as England became the dominant force in the world and acquired all the lands on the east coast between the Mississippi River and the Atlantic Ocean, the face of the emerging nation became distinctly white, Anglo-Saxon and Protestant.

As it grew, the values, ethics and principles of this country were those of conservative Protestantism. In fact, they were decidedly anti-Catholic in some places.[2] The church in this country was largely an immigrant church as it grew in the nineteenth and twentieth centuries. These new arrivals tended naturally to gather in ethnic neighborhoods and churches served by clergy of their own countries and that preserved their native culture and language. It was not that long ago that Catholicism in the United States was largely an urban religion with several churches in any given area. I remember my neighborhood in Denver, which had an Irish Catholic church and an Italian Catholic church within a block of each other. This was typical in most large cities. The churches were fairly large and served both the spiritual and social needs of their people.

As Catholics moved into mainstream America, they became further removed from their immigrant roots, immersed in American culture and not as likely to stay in their old neighborhoods. The church took on a suburban character as well as an urban identity. More and more Catholics moved to more and more diverse areas, and the small parish became a more common occurrence.

Although this is a simplistic overview, it helps highlight some of the important factors in the American Catholic situation as well as some of the influences on small parishes today. The old urban church was well-organized and had several priests and a staff. The laity had little responsibility for the day-to-day events that kept the parish functioning. Many of the priests who became pastors of these small parishes had, and in some places continue to have, only the model of the large urban parish to draw on. Small parishes have had to find their own identities and their own way of operating along the way. The development of lay leadership and liturgy programs is part of that development.

Who Are We Today?

To talk about liturgy in small parishes today we need to talk about the definition of a small parish. It is not defined by numbers alone but also by location, type of community and demographics. Our working definition of 100 families refers to the number of active, registered parishioners who regularly attend and take part in parish functions and contribute to the upkeep of the parish. However, using the figure of 100 families as a beginning definition can be misleading because church census counts usually include many families who have moved, have stopped attending or simply live in the community and were included in a census. It may even include part-time families. My own parish is listed as having over 500 families. In reality, we currently have about 80 active families!

So how do we define a small parish? The location of the parish and the character of that location are also part of the definition. The size and construction of the buildings may be part of the picture, and not only the number of parishioners but who they are, how often they are present and why they are present helps define the small parish.

There are many rural parishes across our country, especially in the heartland and in farming areas. Small towns and villages exist throughout our country, from New England villages to Sunbelt parishes whose populations swell each winter. There are small mining towns and outlying suburbs. Our large cities have shrinking inner-city parishes. Each of these has a distinct personality but shares in the unity of our liturgy.

Resort parishes exist in mountains, by lakes, at the seashore and in our national parks and recreation areas. These may have varying numbers depending on the season. Some are not really parishes but exist to provide a faith community for seasonal workers and thus require the services of a circuit-riding priest. Other resorts have two sets of registered parishioners, one of full-time residents and another of part-time residents who have vacation property in the area.

Our cities have parishes that are now small due to population shifts. Some of them have extensive histories and former populations that were quite large. Now they are faced with shrinking congregations. These parishes still have an identity and a place in their community. In earlier times it was not uncommon for more than one parish to exist in a neighborhood, usually tied to a specific ethnic community that has now dispersed.

Each of these parishes has its own unique identity, problems and solutions to those problems. Rural parishes usually have to be concerned with unpredictable factors such as the weather and farming seasons; often their congregations are scattered over a large geographical area, making frequent committee meetings impractical. Sunbelt parishes must operate in two modes — serving the smaller year-round community and serving the larger winter community whose numbers may or may not be active in parish life. The concerns of the mining community will be different from those of the seashore parish or the small suburban parish, but the needs of all are important.

Resort parishes have to rely on a small number of families who are regular or full-time parishioners to provide hospitality and good liturgy for varying sizes of assemblies. Mountain parishes in particular may also have problems with unpredictable weather. It can be difficult to plan meetings, rehearsals or even liturgies when snow and/or fog conditions may necessitate canceling them at the last minute. Being hospitable also involves planning liturgies that allow visitors to participate fully. For some of these parishes there is also an attitude problem to consider: Many parishioners may be tired of schedules and plans and have moved to the area to escape "big city" pressures. Rigid schedules just won't work. This may also be true of seasonal parishes where many of the parishioners may be retired and not enthusiastic about getting involved.

Small inner-city parishes may have to deal with deteriorating facilities and complex social outreach needs as well as diverse ethnic populations. And they also have the economic problem of having fewer people to cover the costs of operation. Many of these parishes have large old buildings that are in need of repairs or updating and are too large for current needs. Some are in areas of great poverty, with the homeless and hungry looking to them for help. In addition, virtually all small parishes today have the sword of closure hanging over their heads as diocesan offices seek to maximize their resources in an era of fewer and fewer priests.

But each of the problems also offers unique opportunities for the small parish. Being a small community to begin with, people are more likely to know one another and feel a sense of kinship. Reaching out to strangers and being examples of the unity of the Body of Christ is a challenge for resort parishes. For those Catholics who make the effort to attend Mass while on vacation, being welcomed and made to feel a part of the community is a very affirming experience. In those parishes with fluctuating seasonal populations, the ability to be community and to worship together using the diverse gifts that come together with each season can be enriching for all involved. The inner-city parish has the opportunity to reach out and make a difference in its secular community. They also may have the perfect setting to incorporate aspects of different cultures into their liturgies, thereby making them even richer. There are no problems that do not also offer opportunities to grow.

So there really isn't one definition of a small parish. If you are reading this book, you probably identify with some aspect of the definition or the problem. And you are also probably in a position to turn those problems into opportunities. The task isn't as formidable as it seems. Like any other, it requires knowledge and preparation. The good news is that there are resources available to you that will make the job easier and more interesting. A word of warning, however: Good liturgy is habit-forming!

Starting at the Beginning

In constructing a church building, one starts with a solid foundation. The same is true of building a strong liturgy program. There is a foundation of knowledge essential to preparing liturgy. There are those who think that because they have attended Mass for years and years, they know how to prepare liturgy. That is like thinking that because you have eaten gourmet food for years you know how to prepare it. In both cases, the experience is helpful and is a good starting place for further education.

To follow the example of cooking, to learn to prepare meals, a person needs a cookbook. Once the basic principles are understood, the cook can be creative. It is the same with liturgy: Once the principles are understood, the liturgist can be more creative. In preparing liturgy we have a cookbook of sorts, in fact several cookbooks. The liturgy documents of and since Vatican II set out the goals of the church regarding our liturgy and give details on how to accomplish those goals. There are ten documents that deal with liturgy, and all of them are available in one book, *The Liturgy Documents: A Parish Resource*.[3] This book gives not only the documents but also an overview of each one by a scholar in that particular area of the liturgy.

It is important to know the vision of the church for our liturgy, which is set forth in the *Constitution on the Sacred Liturgy* (CSL). For the liturgist, article 10 of the CSL is a touchstone. It states that "the liturgy is the summit toward which the activity of the church is directed; at the same time it is the fount from which all the church's power flows." It is not altar guilds, men's and women's groups, the religious education programs, social outreach activities, Bible study or prayer groups that are the source of strength and growth for a parish. It is the liturgy—in particular the Sunday eucharist, or Mass—that provides the focal point of the parish. This is where we come together as the body of Christ to give praise to God, to be nourished by the body and blood of Christ and to be empowered by the Holy Spirit to take the gospel out into the world. Then all the other activities will flow from the fulfilling of that charge to bring good news to the poor.

If the activities of a parish are the focal point rather than the liturgy, it is a case of the tail wagging the dog. "Unless the Lord builds the house, those who build it labor in vain" (Psalm 127:1). If worship of the Lord is not at the heart of everything we do, we may as well be another social club.

Chapter ten of this book will deal with *The Constitution on the Sacred Liturgy* and other documents of the Second Vatican Council, the sacramentary, the lectionary and the rite books and their role in creating a better understanding of liturgy. It is sufficient to say here that this is essential reading — basic training, as it were — for all who would be responsible for preparing liturgical celebrations. It is important to read all these documents and books thoroughly. As you read other material and attend workshops, you may read or hear quotes from these documents. The quotes may or may not be in context. And even while reading the documents, some sections will seem to contradict each other. More than a casual reading is necessary to understand both the letter of the law and the intent or spirit of the law.

Cooperation

Just as our liturgies do not take place in a vacuum, neither does our preparation. It is a team effort. Here again, the difference between small parishes and larger ones is size — or more precisely, numbers. Our teams may be smaller, but the amount of work is not necessarily less. The leader of the team is your pastor, who also can be a good source of education. Admittedly, some pastors are more knowledgeable than others and some are better teachers, but a mutual respect for the liturgy and for each other opens many avenues of learning for both parties.

If you are fortunate enough to have a deacon in your parish, he is a valuable member of the team. He can also help with your educational process since he, like the pastor, received extensive liturgical formation prior to ordination. Having a deacon changes the shape of your celebrations somewhat, and it is important to understand the deacon's role. By working together, the task of preparing liturgies for your parish becomes easier for everyone. Since small parishes tend to have less support staff for assistance, your pastor is also more likely to be responsive to a fuller approach to liturgy if he knows it isn't going to add to his already too full schedule.

The other staff person to consider is your religious education leader. In a small parish, this person could also be involved in the beginning stages of catechetical formation and you could share resources. Since liturgy must include children — however the parish chooses to do so — communication with the person responsible for education is essential. Finding out on a Sunday morning that there is a special first communion Mass the following Saturday morning can really put a crimp in your day! "We're having first communions next Saturday. Could you do some music for us?"!!

What's wrong with this scene? At the very least, it shows a lack of understanding about the nature of liturgy, not to mention a lack of understanding of the importance of this sacrament in the life of the child and of the community. Not to despair, however, as even this can be the beginning of growth. Some practical solutions to this type of problem will come in later chapters. For now it serves to illustrate the importance of including the religious education program in the liturgical team. Good cooperation makes a more cohesive liturgical program for all.

It is also a good idea to get to know your counterparts at nearby parishes. From a practical standpoint as well as an ecumenical one, getting to know the staff at other churches in your area or town is a good idea. A sharing of ideas and resources is beneficial to all concerned. If you are seeking a specific resource — a book, a vestment, music or something specific for the seasonal environment — you may find help as close as your phone.

This is also true of program resources. Small parishes have fewer people in any ongoing process such as confirmation or RCIA. If we are fortunate, there may be another parish relatively close by, and by joining forces we can enrich each other's programs and lives.

Learning is a lifelong process, no less so in liturgy than in other areas. The old adage that two heads are better than one is certainly true here. By joining with others active in the field of liturgy, the experience of each benefits all. A well-rounded education can only improve your liturgical skills.

The Care and Feeding of Liturgists

Remember that you are more than a liturgist. You are, first of all, a child of God growing in your own spiritual development. A retreat director once reminded me that it is necessary to inhale in order to exhale. While this may seem obvious, we liturgists tend to get so wrapped up in our work that we forget to take time to tend to our own spiritual needs. This leads to burnout, both physically and spiritually. In addition to taking time for personal retreats, workshops and conferences offer a chance for nourishment as well as learning.

If there is a religious education congress or conference in your diocese, or if you are able to attend one in another area, it will certainly be a wonderful experience. People come from all over the United States to attend the one in Los Angeles, for example. The workshops generally cover a wide range of topics, not just "how to" classes for religious education teachers. They generally offer topics ranging from scripture study to personal prayer development and from music and liturgy to moral theology, usually taught by some of the foremost scholars in those fields.

These conferences are also an opportunity to attend large, elaborate liturgies at which those attending are interested participants. The liturgies usually feature some of the best musicians, dancers, artists and homilists in the country. Although these are not the usual or normal style of liturgy, they can be stimulating and spiritually nourishing for you. You may even come away with an inspiration for your own parish.

Many dioceses also sponsor liturgical conferences each year. These conferences focus on various aspects of liturgy and usually feature presenters who are well-known in their fields. It is an occasion to meet with them and with other liturgists to share experiences and ideas, and even horror stories — and they will understand!

One word of caution is in order here. It is not only possible but very probable that you will hear several people speaking on the same topic but giving conflicting opinions. Are they incorrect in their ideas? Occasionally they are, or at least in their interpretation of a particular document. Some of their liturgical practices may be questionable, but this does not negate the benefit of hearing their ideas. It does underscore the importance of your own basic knowledge of liturgical norms. Sometimes it is a matter of size again, and sometimes it is just a different point of view. Nonetheless, once in a while you learn more from someone with whom you disagree. And in order to disagree, you have to reevaluate your own position, looking again at those principles upon which your judgment rests.

Basically, the ministry of liturgist requires a commitment of time and effort that few people who aren't "behind the scenes" can appreciate. You can use all the help you can get, whether it be education or assistance from other people. Enthusiasm is contagious, and results create enthusiasm. So by including as many opportunities for education and cooperation in your ministry as possible, you add a lift not only to yourself but to those you serve and those with whom you work.

●

1 Vincent Branick, The House Church in the Writings of Paul *(Wilmington, DE: Michael Glazier, Inc., 1989), 20.*

2 *For an excellent picture of Catholicism in the development of this country, see "The Church in the United States." In chapter 22 of William Bausch,* Pilgrim Church *(Mystic, CT: Twenty-third Publications, 1981). I am indebted to him for most of my understanding and material on this subject.*

3 *Elizabeth Hoffman, ed.,* The Liturgy Documents: A Parish Resource, *3rd ed. (Chicago: Liturgy Training Publications, 1981).*

Chapter Two

Mining the Treasure

Where Is the Knowledge?

Finding your parish resources is like mining for treasure. It takes a lot of digging, but the rewards can be very worthwhile. One of the first steps is to discover who knows what. In every parish there is at least one person who has been there since Noah got off the ark! These people know everyone who has ever been part of the parish, every activity that ever existed, and who is able and willing to help. In addition, they will probably be flattered that they have been asked.

Our senior citizens really are the elders of our communities, and too often their knowledge is dismissed. They have weathered many changes in their lifetimes, and we can learn much from their faith and wisdom. In some small parishes these elders may have been responsible for the existence of the parish and the building of the church. In our parish, for example, there are still several members who were not only present at the beginning of our parish but who physically built the building we now occupy. Some of these elders have told stories of meeting in the meadow of a campground for a time before the building was ready! They are the living history of our parish community.

Another very important resource is your pastor. As we mentioned in the last chapter, he can be of educational assistance. Additionally, if he has a real interest in liturgy, your enthusiasm and support may enable him to venture into more creative areas. It can be very difficult for a pastor who must care for the needs of his people, coordinate all the parish's activities, administer his parish, pay the bills and write a fresh and exciting homily each week to get very enthusiastic about adding to his burden. Until he knows he can count on you to work as part of a team and finish what you start, he may not seem eager to put new ideas into practice. Who knows — perhaps your interest and enthusiasm will refresh his own liturgical spirit.

Music is yet another resource that can be very helpful. Does your parish have someone in charge of the music program? What is this person's level of skill and knowledge? Since music is not an option but an essential, this is someone with whom you as a liturgist must work very closely. If it is someone who has keyboard skills and little liturgical background, you may be able to learn together. If it is someone who does have some training in liturgy, this person can be a great help in putting together a coordinated liturgical approach for your parish.

In chapter one we mentioned neighboring parish liturgists. While not exactly a parish resource, they can, nonetheless, be of help. They may know of workshops and seminars coming to your area, and by pooling your people and theirs might make it a more enjoyable and educational day for all. The same is true of printed material. Since most publishers give a better price for larger quantities, perhaps you could cooperate in ordering materials and stretch each other's liturgical dollars. Some rural parishes share their pastor or their musician. In this case, knowing your counterpart will be even more helpful, and it can not only make liturgy in both parishes better but also make life a little easier for your pastor.

Musicians from other churches in your community can also be a helpful resource. They may know accompanists in your area who are available if needed. Copies of special music can be shared among churches in some instances. It never hurts to have a friend involved in liturgical ministry to help you keep abreast of happenings in other churches in your community. Through this avenue, it is possible to exchange not only ideas but also knowledge.

You will find that we have much in common with our Christian neighbors. Working together, especially on music, is not only educational but fun. If your community does not have an ecumenical Thanksgiving service, this would be a good opportunity for your churches to get to know one another. Community programs of Christmas carols are also popular. Ecumenical outreach can be very enriching for everyone involved.

What Is Your History?

Every parish has a history. We have histories, and we have traditions. By using that knowledge of our histories and past traditions, we can build on them and be sure that the best gets handed on. This is an area in which the parish elders we spoke of can be of great help. They can remember how Holy Week has been celebrated over the years or where the Nativity set originated. They can tell you the history of your church organ or altar or that special statue out front. Their knowledge can help prevent you from inadvertently changing something that has been an important part of worship in your parish for many years. Even some practices which aren't, strictly speaking, liturgically correct may need to be preserved in some way. If you understand both the liturgical principles and the pastoral needs involved, you will be able to be sensitive to both. That sensitivity will gain you much-needed cooperation from those who might otherwise feel threatened.

Does your parish have some non-liturgical traditions you need to be aware of, such as an annual picnic or New Year's Eve celebration? What about special devotions? If the liturgy has not been the fount from which everything else in your parish flows, you need to know where the water has been coming from! It is easier, and more pastoral, if you are able to build the liturgical component into existing traditions as you grow toward the ideal of eucharistic celebrations being the summit of parish life. While we know that there is more to parish life than bingo, it may take a while to pass that along to your community. Patience, creativity, sensitivity and a lot of prayer help smooth the way.

In addition to learning what has been done in the past, it is very important to learn *who* did it. Not only will they be a source of information and help, but not knowing about them could create an embarrassing situation for you. No one likes to be overlooked after doing a job for years (or even just months). If Agnes has scheduled the lectors for the last several years, it would be a good idea to consult her about adding lectors and initiating a training program for them before going ahead. Most of us don't walk into a situation where no one has done anything but come to Mass. Every parish has a history, and that history is people. The community is the church. We don't do anything "to" them, only "with" them. As liturgists, our role is to facilitate the relationship between God and people in worship. Sensitivity to your community and its history is essential.

In one of my first small parish experiences, we were planning Holy Week when I proceeded to tell the assembled committee how many lectors would be needed and gave some suggestions on how to recruit them. One member of the group quickly pointed out, somewhat indignantly, that he had lectors already and had been scheduling them for some time. In other words, we're not total dopes here, you know. Oops! Remove foot from mouth and start over; painful lesson learned — be sure to know who has been doing what before jumping ahead with plans. It took a while to reestablish that relationship!

So among your first tasks is finding out what has been done in past years, both in and out of liturgy. Who were the people involved? Did it work? What things were successful and what things flopped? By talking to those who did the work, you can get an idea of how your community prays and plays together. They can give you a pretty good picture of the strengths and weaknesses with which you will be working. And you will be seen as one who listens, not as the one who just wants to come in and change everything.

Where Is the Talent?

In these discussions with your pastor, your elders and others who have been working and ministering, you will get an idea of the talents in your community. Ask for suggestions of people to become lectors or eucharistic ministers. Listen for good voices in the assembly who may be potential choir members. Watch for those with good people skills and for the natural leaders.

In building a liturgy program there are many components, and it is not possible to deal with all of them at the same time. A liturgy committee and program doesn't spring into being fully functional overnight. But by building ministry by ministry, all will be strengthened as each is strengthened. Evaluate what is in place. Do you have enough lectors now, or do you need a specific design to recruit and train people? Are there enough eucharistic ministers? If you aren't already receiving communion under both species, how can you make this come about? What about cantors or choir?

Recruiting ministers always seems to be a formidable task. Notices in the bulletin sometimes work, but most of the time it takes a personal touch. Many people are just waiting to be asked. There also may be people serving in a particular ministry who would love a chance to change. Father may have asked Martha to be a lector years ago, and she didn't want to say no; but now she is tired and no longer particularly effective at proclaiming. Joe may have been taking up the collection for as long as anyone can remember, but he longs to be a eucharistic minister. No one ever asked, and he didn't think it was appropriate to volunteer. Many people won't volunteer for fear of being rejected, or they don't think they are "worthy" of being a minister. It takes patience and love to help them see that through Jesus Christ, they are worthy and able to minister in his name.

It is especially difficult to recruit young people, but it is also especially important to recruit them. They are a part of our parish but don't always feel that they are part of it. They bring a fresh vitality to our liturgies, a sense of future. If you have a youth group, meet with them. Let them know that you want them to participate in ministry as well as in the Mass. They are part of the Body of Christ, too, and their presence adds vitality to any community.

If your local high school has a speech or drama department, see if any of your youth are involved and invite them to share their talent as lectors. Check with the music department for singers and instrumentalists. One of the greatest experiences with my choir was with a young man who played bassoon and clarinet. I gave him copies of our music and invited him to join us. For the next three years Steven helped us create beautiful music with his talent. He was a faithful choir member and brought an innovative sound and support to our small group. At an age when many young people stop attending Mass, this young man had almost perfect attendance! We truly missed him when he went on to the university.

When people feel genuinely needed and that their talents are appreciated, it is much easier to fill ministerial roles, both the public ones at Mass or those behind the scenes, such as art and environment. In a small parish, we need to consider our numbers. Some people may fill more than one ministry. But we also need to be cautious about not overloading people. It is very easy to keep going to the same people we know to be reliable, but this isn't fair either to them or to those whom we don't ask. We may be overlooking that one person who has just the right talent, if only they knew they were needed.

But I Don't Know How

One of the most common excuses for not being involved is "I don't know how." As liturgists, it is our task to show people how. We first need to match the right person to the right ministry. Pushing a very shy person to do a very public task is not fair. Some people who are shy are able to be very effective lectors, just as some shy people make good actors. But if someone is uncomfortable speaking in public, training may not help. This is where getting to know your people is important. Someone who may not be comfortable in the role of lector may be the perfect person to train as a sacristan or to do some portion of that job. Not every singer is able to be a cantor or a soloist in the choir. But the more involved people become in the liturgical function of a parish, the more they own it. The liturgy becomes a part of them. Then the Mass and their faith ceases to be a "Sunday thing" and becomes an integral part of their lives. This is what community — being the Body of Christ — is all about.

Another problem arises when a person who volunteers for a ministry doesn't have the skills necessary. This is a very delicate area, and it is important not to devalue anyone. However, it is necessary to evaluate skills and to be ready to suggest (tactfully) another area of need that is more appropriate. The specific ministries and the skills needed are discussed in greater detail in a later chapter.

Once someone has volunteered for a ministry, training is vital. A lector needs to be able to do more than just read aloud. Scripture is proclaimed — not read — and requires a different approach. Choir members may be able to sing but not know how to read music. That is all right when they begin, but learning to read music should then become part of rehearsal.

Basic liturgical knowledge and skills are necessary for any minister. It is easy to think that because they receive communion each week, people will know what to do as eucharistic ministers. Even the best-trained people go blank under stress. Presiders need the words in front of them, even though they may know the prayers and responses by heart. It is very important to train each of your ministers not just to know their function but to be comfortable in their role.

There are options for this training. Some dioceses offer annual training workshops in specific ministries. There are workshops conducted by professionals for single parishes or for groups of parishes. If you or your pastor or deacon is comfortable with it, the training can be done in your own parish by any or all of you. You also can contact the office for worship in your diocese for assistance.

At our parish, we have all our ministers gather for a day of training. This day begins with some basic liturgical training, because all ministers should have an understanding of the liturgy. (Most of us stop religious education after confirmation, and liturgy isn't a big subject even then.) This training takes the form of a workshop with lectures and questions and answers. This is followed by lunch and a hands-on workshop in a specific ministry in the afternoon. Eucharistic ministers get to practice where to stand, how to offer the cup, how to offer the bread and how to clean up after communion. We also go over those things that can best be described as the choreography of the liturgy — where to stand, how to move and how to get from point A to point B. It sounds simple — and it is — but people are more comfortable if they know exactly what they are to do.

We do the same thing with training the lectors. They have a chance to rehearse the entrance procession carrying the book, to practice going to the ambo and to actually proclaim the scriptures. This gives them a chance to learn microphone skills. We have used a video camera for this portion of the workshop very effectively. None of us likes to see ourselves on camera, but it is the only way to really know how we look and sound. Our lectors' skills improved dramatically after the video workshop.

The need for training is also true of ushers, altar servers and ministers of hospitality. Being comfortable in a role is essential to doing it well. It is also easier to recruit ministers if they know they will receive training and not just be thrown into the task. No one wants to be embarrassed by making an error. Serving at Mass is serious and can be intimidating for the inexperienced minister.

We try to have an annual workshop for our ministers. This gives us a chance to train new people and gives experienced people a chance to share their knowledge with the newcomers. We all learn from each other. It is also a chance to see if there are any problems with procedures that need to be corrected and a chance to make any needed changes in the routine. Sometimes the most thought-out choreography doesn't work in practice, or someone will have something new to offer from a workshop or a different parish they have attended. We encourage all our ministers to attend the local religious education congress each year and to observe what is done in other parishes. Growth generally results in change, and because we hope our ongoing training results in growth, we need to make provisions for change.

Each ministry has different training needs. Obviously the musicians have rehearsals, but they also benefit from the liturgical portion of such a workshop. If you have a bereavement ministry, it has its own unique necessary training. The same is true of preparing couples for marriage or for the baptism of their children. The ministry for initiation of adults (RCIA) has still other training needs. But all of these ministers need to develop a real understanding of liturgy and how their ministry is part of the liturgical experience.

Each of these special ministries — bereavement, marriage preparation, baptism, RCIA — has its own special liturgies, and those involved need to receive training in the basic principles and structures of their area of specialization. In a small parish there is bound to be some overlap of people involved in more than one ministry, but they all need to be aware that the same principles of liturgy that apply to Sunday Mass also apply to weddings, funerals, baptisms and the liturgies connected to the RCIA.

This may sound like a lot of ministries — more than you have the resources or need for in your parish. But the preceding list is only an example. Depending on the size and needs of your parish, some ministries may be filled by the same people. In our parish we have very few weddings and very few funerals, so the liturgy team prepares what is needed. RCIA is another area where fewer people may be needed. At one workshop I attended, we were given examples of RCIA teams from other parishes, and they had more people on their teams than we have at our Vigil Mass!

But the training in each area is still needed. In our small parishes it just means that some people will be trained in more than one field. Perhaps this will assist them in better understanding how each ministry is connected to the others and to the liturgy as a whole. This is an example of how small parish ministries sometimes have an advantage. Individual ministers don't get lost in the crowd.

Another reason for gathering at least once a year is for spiritual nourishment. Ministry is prayer as well as service. If we are to grow in our ministry, we also need to be fed in our spiritual life. A day of recollection and prayer is a fine gift to give your ministers, done either by your pastor or by an outside source. It is rather like a mini-retreat, and sometimes a retreat master from outside the parish is just what is needed to recharge spiritual batteries. Especially in a small parish, the tendency is to overwork ourselves and our people. This is out of the desire to have the best liturgies we can with fewer people to do the work. But if we don't take care of ourselves spiritually, it can lead to burnout. And that is not in anyone's best interest. People who pray often are better connected to their role in liturgy, and their liturgical role can help them become better in prayer.

The Next Step

In building a liturgical program, as in raising children, the hardest step is letting go. Early in your thinking, it is important to be able to delegate and become a coordinator of the planning and preparations of others. If you run the whole show, others don't have any ownership interest in the process and soon will have no commitment, either. The old adage about doing a job yourself if you want it done right is a deadly error, and you will soon find yourself doing everything. This certainly doesn't build community or strengthen faith. Instead, it will wear you out and in the long run alienate you from those you are seeking to serve.

The best teacher is one who helps others gain the knowledge, means and opportunity to help others grow. Teach the skill, impart the knowledge, then let the students become teachers also. One of the true joys in this work is to watch others become enthusiastic and acquire the ability to get the job done. If your parish liturgy can't run without you, you haven't done your job. That doesn't mean you work yourself out of a job, only that it changes. Instead of drawing the liturgical picture and filling in the blanks, you will become the weaver who takes the threads of talent around you and creates a tapestry. Each thread has its own color and texture and its own place in the picture. As a coordinator, you help pull all those threads together.

Be aware that others might not do things the way you would, and that this is all right because there is more than one way to accomplish a goal. This is where a thorough understanding of the principles of liturgy and their pastoral implications is important. It allows more flexibility. People learning anything, including ministry, need the freedom to make their own mistakes and to learn from them. As your people grow, the liturgy in your parish becomes uniquely its own, filling the needs of your particular set of circumstances.

If it doesn't do violence to the structure of the liturgy, allow the space necessary for growth. When I first started working on art and environment in the worship space, banners were a big item. We had banners for every season. We had banners with cute sayings and pictures, banners on the walls, banners on processional poles, banners everywhere! As those of us working in this area grew into a better understanding of the function of environmental decor, we were able to use banners and other fabric decor more simply and less often. Was the first approach wrong? No — it was part of the growth process. Would I do it that way now? Again, no — but I would certainly allow someone just getting involved in this ministry the creative freedom to go through the same growth process. Perhaps with the guidance I didn't have they might reach a better understanding of their ministry more quickly, but creativity is what keeps us fresh and relevant. Make no mistake — liturgy and creativity go hand in hand.

The goal is for you to be able to step back and breathe. You do have a life outside of church (if not, something is wrong), and you need the time and space to fulfill other needs. By learning to delegate and enable others to take their places in the liturgical scheme, your parish can only be a better place to work and worship.

●

CHAPTER 3

Like Pulling Teeth

Take Them Where They Are

Catechesis for the assembly is a vital part of forming a solid liturgical program. It is a given that not everyone in your community is knowledgeable about matters of liturgy. Most people haven't read any of the documents of Vatican II or the specific liturgy documents that came from them. For the most part, in my experience, people's knowledge of liturgy comes from their history of Mass attendance. If they have experienced the full richness of the Mass in the past, they may have a better recognition and appreciation of its beauty. If, however, their experience is primarily that of a minimalist style of liturgy, that limited form is their understanding of the appropriate way to celebrate.

Making changes to that way of celebrating can be like pulling teeth — difficult and painful. But catechesis is a very effective anesthetic that both eases the way and reduces the pain. It can make the difference between entrenched resistance and enthusiasm for new ideas.

It is also a given that not everyone is going to be enthusiastic about changes to their style of worship. Change can be very unsettling for most of us; it is a threat to the stability most people look for in their lives. When so much in our world is changing at lightning speed, the stability of the Mass is like a security blanket for many. Here, at least, they know what to expect.[1]

To some extent we are still suffering from the overnight changes in the Mass after Vatican II. There was little, if any, catechesis for most people. One Sunday, Mass was in Latin, the priest had his back to the people and private prayers and praying the rosary during Mass were normal and acceptable. The next Sunday, Mass was in the vernacular, the altar and priest were facing the people, and the people were expected to participate in the prayers and songs. They were even asked to touch each other by shaking hands during the sign of peace! Many of the priests made these changes with little catechesis and with even less enthusiasm. These abrupt changes caused much pain and resentment to many of our brothers and sisters, and that pain and resentment often has lasted to this day.

To be sensitive to these needs for stability and to past painful change, it is necessary to take the time to know the worship history of the parish. How open are they to new ideas? Is there already a conflict between generations or between longtime members and newcomers? Where are the areas of mutual agreement or cooperation within the parish? In his keynote address to the 1994 National Association of Pastoral Musicians Conference on Rural Parishes, Dr. Bernard Evans commented that a major problem for rural parishes is the distrust between those who have recently arrived from cities and the long-standing members of a community.

It is important to remember that this is their parish, too. They have a right to be able to worship without a sense of conflict. They also have a right to the best and fullest liturgy possible. Reconciling these needs is part of the job of the liturgist, and catechesis is at the heart of that reconciliation.

When people have an understanding of why something you want to change is important, they are more likely to be willing to give it a try. If they feel they have a role in that change, they can make it a part of themselves and can own it. That knowledge and ownership leads to enthusiasm, and enthusiasm creates a sense of openness where God can make changes in lives and communities. These changes may surprise you. After all, God is the author of creation, and change is part of that creation.

Patience Is a Virtue

We have heard the phrase "patience is a virtue" so often that it is easy to dismiss it as just another hackneyed phrase. But it does take patience to build a strong participating community. It is important to let people catch up. Abrupt and total change leads to disaster.

As I mentioned earlier, when I first became a liturgist in a small parish, the first thing we had to plan was Holy Week. Having experienced Holy Week as the high point of the liturgical year in my former large parish, I was determined that these good people should also have this experience. So the plans were made by going over the rituals called for in the sacramentary with the local priest. Stepping in for the ill choir director (of a choir of six people), I planned all the music very carefully so that it would be the most effective possible. Of course, no one had ever heard my selections, but we rehearsed all during Lent and had the music pretty well in hand. Every detail of every ritual was looked at and worked out. The needed people were recruited and rehearsed. There was even a well-written and thorough explanation of the Triduum printed in the bulletin (and everyone reads and understands such detailed explanations, of course!)

In my former parish, if you did not arrive early for the Triduum services, you would end up having to stand; the church was full. Imagine my surprise when 30 people showed up for Holy Thursday! And twelve of them were having their feet washed! It being Holy Thursday, we had both wine and bread for communion — in abundance, I might add. To be sure we had enough to serve the large crowd anticipated, a whole bottle of wine was in the flask, much to the dismay of the eucharistic ministers after the service. Good Friday had even fewer people. Holy Saturday saw a slight increase in the size of the assembly, to about 50! The fire was magnificent, the readings were well done, the choir did their part as rehearsed, and all the bells and smells proclaimed this as high ritual indeed.

Easter morning saw the church filled and overflowing into additional seating. It was also a full liturgy, but not to the same extent as Saturday's Vigil. In evaluating the services, people did not understand the Triduum and thought it was silly. After all, Easter is on Sunday, not Thursday, Friday or Saturday. This was liturgy done to and for them, not with them. In essence, it was the strangers from the big city telling them they didn't know what they were doing. Rather than a worship experience, there was resentment.

Too much, too fast and you lose. I can look back at that experience now and laugh, but there is also the pain of arrogance. There was no sensitivity to the people. There were the best of intentions, but no sensitivity and no opportunity for the people to understand and own these rituals. So the rituals had little meaning for them.

We left that parish not long after. Because of this lack of sensitivity, I no longer had credibility and could not effectively bring about any change. But I thank God for the experience. It was painful but also humbling and very educational. There is no shame in making mistakes, and this was neither the first nor the last. Shame comes from being too arrogant to admit the mistake and learn from it.

It really is important not to just have book knowledge of how to do the right rituals and why to do them and when to do them. You must also know your brothers and sisters and respect where they are in their lives. What are their pains, their joys, their needs? How, with the tools you have, can you assist them in their journey to God? The liturgical laws are not meant to beat people over the head but to lead them to a fuller participation in giving glory to God and growing in the fullness of their faith.

Catechesis — A Growth Experience

While catechesis usually involves starting at the beginning, it is an ongoing process. Just as your own education in liturgy builds on previous knowledge, what you pass along to your assembly builds. It is never possible to sit back and say, "Now they know all they need." For one thing, most communities are not static, so there are always new people who will learn new things. The good news is that much of what you teach will be taught to new people by those who have already learned. Knowledge is much like dropping a stone in a pond: The ripples keep expanding throughout the entire body of water.

There is no one way to catechize a community. Bulletin notes can be effective for some things. A weekly liturgy corner that breaks down the Mass into its parts and explains their function, history and relationship to the other parts is a helpful tool, but each article must be short and easily understood. This isn't the place for detailed theological discussions. Special seasonal bulletin inserts detailing aspects of that season are also a good idea. The Triduum bulletin insert mentioned earlier wasn't a bad idea, it was just too much to absorb in one season with no other sources of information. I've used the same bulletin insert several years in a row, using it to reinforce teaching sessions for various ministries as well as to help explain the reasons for these special rituals. But the rituals grew over the years so that each year, the bulletin articles became more meaningful.

If change is done more slowly — if rituals are introduced with some type of instruction — people can see how they fit into the liturgy. It would be nice to come in and wave a wand over the community, instantly transforming it into the vision of perfection. But life just isn't that neat, and your vision of perfection may not be (and probably should not be) the vision of those around you! The ideal is the goal, but the possible is reality.

One of the more successful means of catechesis in our parish has involved small groups. Each time there is a day of training for any of the ministries, it includes catechesis and not just "job training." We try to relate something of the history of our church, especially as it relates to a specific ministry. How did this ministry begin, and how has it grown and changed over the centuries? How does it relate to the liturgy as a whole? In which part of the Mass does this ministry take place, and what is the history and significance of that part?

Another very appropriate way of teaching is to gather the participants for special liturgies that allow them to rehearse. No one is comfortable just being thrown into a job, even if it is carrying a candle in a procession. Taking time to explain not only how to do what is being asked but why goes a long way toward successfully implementing plans. And this time can also be used to explain more about what is being celebrated and why.

Great Triduum celebrations in our parish began to take place when we gathered everyone who would be taking part — ushers, lectors, eucharistic ministers, those having their feet washed, altar servers — and before beginning individual rehearsals spent a few minutes giving a brief overview of the significance of these holy days and their history in the early church. Rather than being bored, people hung on every word. They said afterward that they had never known what these three days meant or why they were important. And they wanted to know more. The bulletin insert was read with new interest that year, and attendance went way up. The enthusiasm has continued to this day, and we have been able to expand the ritual so that it truly is the high point of our community's liturgical year.

Other teachable moments include the planning for baptisms and weddings, and even for funerals, although to a lesser extent. Special sessions for parents prior to the baptism of their children are a time to explain not only what it is they are undertaking with this sacrament but the ritual that goes with it. This does two things: It makes them more comfortable during the rite — knowing where to go and when and what to do — and it helps them see that there is meaning behind the ritual. It isn't just words and water. The symbols have much deeper meanings and a long history.

The same is true for helping a couple plan their wedding liturgy. A set of rigidly imposed rules for weddings only leads to resentment and frustration, but an explanation of the ritual and the possibilities for making the ceremony meaningful and personal for them as a couple can be the opening for them to begin looking at their spiritual life in marriage. Unfortunately, planning the actual liturgy is usually the last thing a couple does, and many decisions may already have been made. This is an area that requires not only knowledge and skill but also patience and diplomacy.

It is a sad fact that wedding customs in this country don't fit well with sacramental liturgy. Change in this area comes slowly, but success begets success. As young people experience the beauty of well-executed sacramental wedding liturgies, their ideas of a traditional wedding change. For most of us, the ideal wedding is what we see in movies and in bridal magazines — a fairy tale that has little relationship to the new life being entered. Marriage preparation must look at the rites of the ceremony as well as at the new life of the couple as husband and wife. We need to help them see the connection.

Good liturgy can be the best of all the forms of catechesis. When the pastor, the liturgist, the musicians and all the other ministers are all working together in a coordinated fashion, the rituals and symbols speak for themselves very powerfully. Your and your pastor's efforts in teaching those who are responsible for various parts of the liturgy will bear fruit with the community as a whole. Be creative, be knowledgeable, be enthusiastic and be patient.

Get Them Involved

People need to be needed. One of the best ways to improve a liturgy program is to get people involved. This cannot be just token involvement — get them involved in ways that are meaningful. When you ask someone to do a job, make it plain that you are counting on them. Then give them the training they need, and step back. Be sure also that there really is a job to do. I once went to help with a Passion play after being asked by the pastor, who told me he really needed me to do a specific job. When I arrived, someone else was doing that job, had been doing so for other plays, and didn't know why I was there. I was not as quick to respond to that pastor's requests for help after that.

As was mentioned in an earlier chapter, not everyone has the same talents. But everyone can do something. Processions are a great way to get people involved. Ordinary Time usually calls for a simple entrance procession, but major feasts and solemnities call for more celebratory processions. These can include people with banners, candles, flowers or whatever else is appropriate to the season and to your community. There are many areas of liturgy in which the ritual not only allows but calls for creativity.

Another good way to involve people is to have them bring the gifts to the altar. It is quite common to have a family do this and can be a meaningful experience if they know ahead of time that this will be their job. It also can be a chance to teach children something about that part of the liturgy and to feel they are part of the community. It can inspire good spiritual preparation for those involved.

A word of caution, however. We must understand the term "family" in ways other than the traditional family unit of Mom, Dad and their children. All ministries need to reflect the makeup of the community as a whole. Today's communities also consist of single-parent families, single people, unmarried couples, grandparents with grandchildren, widows and widowers. Don't overlook non-traditional family units. In this act of bringing up the gifts, the entire community is represented. So those asked need to reflect the community.

This presentation of the gifts is another part of the liturgy that lends itself well to expansion at specific times. At Masses around Thanksgiving, for example, gifts of food for the poor may be brought up with the bread and wine. In coordination with your religious education program, the children may offer gifts of prayers or good deeds for the community written on cards or on slips of paper placed in a basket. These could be offered at this time by a procession of children before the bread and wine are offered. (Remember, though, that nothing except the appropriate linens, candles, vessels and the bread and wine should be placed on the altar itself.)

Some parishes have two or three people prepare the altar before the gifts are brought forward. They bring out and place the linens, candles and vessels, thus setting the table of the Lord. This is not only a meaningful moment but also a chance to involve more people. If this is, or becomes, a custom in your parish, it can also be expanded for major feasts to include bringing flowers or candles for the altar area. One particularly good time for this is Holy Thursday. You can start with a fairly stark sanctuary, such as you had during Lent, and during the preparation of the gifts transform the area into a more celebratory one for this special celebration of the eucharist.

There are many ways of involving people in more regular ways. Some of these would take some pressure off other ministers. A music librarian for the choir would organize the music for rehearsals, file it away after use and in general keep track of things so that the right music was ready when needed. This may be someone who doesn't sing but loves music and would be a great help to the choir director. The person who coordinates and schedules the lectors or eucharistic ministers doesn't need to be one of these ministers. The sacristy offers the opportunity to perform many small tasks, both regular and sporadic. Perhaps someone could be in charge of keeping the silver polished or the linens washed and ironed. Each task done is an opportunity not only for involvement and a sense of belonging but is also an opportunity to expand people's knowledge and appreciation of the beautiful traditions we call liturgy.

Another way to involve people is to involve their children. One of the joys of being a parent is the pride that comes from watching children accomplish certain tasks. When children are involved in a procession or presentation, attendance always improves! This also has the advantage of making the children realize that they, too, are part of the community and have gifts to offer. Watching a young child bring up the gifts of bread and wine always touches me. Their sense of awe reminds me that we should all be able to approach our Lord with such childlike awe and innocence.

Having children involved usually does mean a certain amount of uncertainty and chaos, but with a little rehearsal and the assistance of a few adults on the side, they add a spark to any liturgy. For our Christmas Eve liturgy last year, we planned to have the children bring the baby Jesus in and place him in the manger, then sing a song. We are a mountain parish with uncertain weather that results in uncertain attendance, so we really couldn't rehearse this. So at the appropriate moment, we asked all the children present to meet the presider in the back of the church and bring baby Jesus to his crib. About 25 kids of all ages joined in the procession as the assembly sang. Then we asked the children to sing "Away in a Manger" with a little help from the women's voices in the choir. Yes, it was a bit disorganized, but it was a touching moment, and more importantly, the baby in the manger became something tangible for these children. We refer to the eucharist as a meal, and so it is. But in small parishes it is often more like a family meal than a formal banquet.

Allowing people to own their liturgy, helping them understand and appreciate what we are doing when we gather and getting them actively involved is what being a liturgist is all about. And that is true no matter what the size of your parish. Those of us in small parishes just have to be a bit more inventive. Catechesis is an ongoing process, but don't be surprised if you learn more than you teach.

●

1 *In his keynote address to the 1994 National Pastoral Musicians Conference on Rural Parishes, Dr. Bernard Evans points out that one major problem with small parishes is resistance to change. Dr. Evans occupies the Virtil Michael Chair in Rural Social Ministries at Saint John's University in Collegeville, Minnesota.*

The Priesthood
of Believers

All Are Called

"All in the assembly gathered for the Mass have an individual right and duty to contribute their participation in ways differing according to the diversity of their order and liturgical function."[1]

In planning any liturgy program for your parish, it is imperative to keep this article in mind. It is not only your goal but your justification for those who doubt that "just anybody" can be a minister. Everyone has not only a right to contribute but a duty to do so.

Putting into action this concept that it is everyone's right and duty to contribute to the liturgy requires overcoming centuries of tradition. In times past, only the priest was regarded as the holy one in the midst of the assembly. Only the priest, by virtue of his ordination, could be a minister. Vatican II decreed that "Such participation by the Christian people as a 'chosen race, a royal priesthood, a holy nation, God's own people' (1 Peter 2:9, see 2:4 – 5) is their right and duty by reason of their baptism."[2] There are two distinct categories of priesthood for Catholics: the ordained priest (or deacon), who ministers those duties reserved for the clergy, and the lay person (also a priest, though not ordained), who ministers those duties that do not require ordination.

"In addition, the ministerial priesthood puts into its proper light another reality of which much should be made, namely, the royal priesthood of believers."[3] The priesthood of believers is the entire Body of Christ, from which the ordained ministers are called forth for the specific role of ministerial priest. But it is also the source of all other ministries. Nearly every document concerning today's Roman Catholic liturgy that came out of Vatican II emphasizes this role of the laity. The *General Instruction of the Roman Missal* (GIRM) tells us that lay people "may perform all the functions below those reserved to deacons."[4] There is a section of the *Constitution on the Sacred Liturgy,* "Norms Drawn from the Hierarchic and Communal Nature of the Liturgy" (Article IIIB), that is very specific on the role of the laity in liturgy. Among other comments, this section tells us that "liturgical services are not private functions" (#26) and that various ministries "exercise a genuine liturgical function" (#29).

Having all these citations won't result in automatic acceptance of any liturgical program you wish to begin, but at least you will have a sound basis for your recommendations. By using these resources, those with whom you are working will know that your ideas aren't your opinions but are grounded in "official" sources. Sometimes being able to remove the personal aspect from your suggestions makes it easier for others to accept them.

As mentioned before, a sound liturgical program doesn't spring into being overnight. It is important to take the time to assess what is currently being done and how well it is being done. Where are improvements needed, and what additional ministries need to be implemented? Then a step-by-step plan can be worked out with your pastor and any others working with you.

The committee approach is very popular, and there are books and seminars on forming liturgy committees. In my experience, these are exercises in futility for a small parish, especially in the beginning stages. The members of your parish who are knowledgeable in liturgical matters need first to form a plan or goal, or perhaps a mission statement, of what you would like to see happening in your parish. What time frame do you see as reasonable for this plan? Then you can bring other leaders on board and train them in specific areas of ministry. As these leaders are trained, you build a liturgy committee working for the same things with a sound base of knowledge from which to work.

If there is a functioning lector program in your parish, for example, start with the person leading that ministry. By including him or her in the plans for that program and gaining their perspective and cooperation, you can work together toward your goals. We will discuss individual ministries in more detail later, but each ministry will have someone who is, at least nominally, the leader. That person has shown an interest in that particular ministry and thus provides a starting point for involvement in its improvement.

How do you build and improve liturgical ministries? Training, training, training, and then more training. There is no way to over-emphasize the importance of giving those who minister the tools they need. This begins with the person who will lead or oversee that particular ministry. That individual needs to have as much knowledge as possible about that particular ministry and know how it relates to the liturgy as a whole. That doesn't mean that he or she will learn it all overnight or that a program can't go forward until all that knowledge is in place. But the leaders do need the basic information so that they can build from that. Liturgical Press and Liturgy Training Publications have excellent resources on the various ministries that explain the ministries, their duties, their history and theology, and provide practical suggestions.[5] They are also valuable tools for training individual ministers.

Using published references also demonstrates that what you are teaching is accepted teaching and not your personal whim. These books are from well-known publishers and are written by people with extensive education and experience in their field, so they are more easily believed. This reading also tends to spark interest in learning more. Once people are interested, half the battle is won.

Specific Ministries

Having discussed the many ministries that go into a parish's liturgical program, we will now discuss each of those ministries more specifically. What are they, and what resources are available for training people to do them? In this section are listed the most common ministries, not necessarily in order of importance — all the ministries are important — but in order of necessity. The exception is the ministry of music. That ministry is so primary to good liturgy and so much more complex that it will be covered by itself in the next chapter.

Lectors "In liturgical celebration each one, minister or lay person, who has an office to perform, should do all of, but only, those parts which pertain to that office by the nature of the rite and the principles of liturgy."[6] Among other citations in various liturgy documents, this serves to highlight that the priest cannot do everything in the Mass. He ought not proclaim the scriptures except for the gospel. Hence, this is listed as the most necessary of ministries.

Since Vatican II, most parishes have had some type of lector program, even if it consists only of the presider, just before Mass, asking someone to read. While this may get the job done, it certainly is not what the liturgy documents have in mind. *The General Instruction of the Roman Missal* tells us that the scripture readings "lay the table of God's word for the faithful and open up the riches of the Bible to them" (#34). The lector is God's storyteller.

In my beginning training sessions for lectors, I tell them to liken our scripture readings at Mass to the family reunion at which everyone gathers and retells family stories — i.e., "Remember when cousin Billy pushed Mary Ann into the lake?" or "Remember how Grandma was always losing her glasses?" These are the stories that hold us together as a family. In the same way, the scriptures tell the story of our Christian family. So lectors have the responsibility of knowing those stories and being able to tell them in ways that bring them to life for the assembly.[7]

There are many tools available to help your lectors become more proficient. One of the best is *Workbook for Lectors and Gospel Readers,* published annually by Liturgy Training Publications.[8] It includes excellent introductions by well-respected liturgists and theologians as well as explanatory comments and suggestions for emphasis, pauses and breathing for each reading. It can be a great help not only to the lectors but also to the presider. In order to do their ministry well, lectors must become at home in the word. They must take the time to read and reflect and make the stories their own. *Workbook* gives practical suggestions, but there are many other resources for scripture study that can also add a deeper understanding of the word of God to the practical demands of the ministry.

What has just been said applies to all lectors in all parishes regardless of size. However, smaller parishes have far fewer people and have to be more creative with our resources. It is not uncommon for one person to be involved in more than one ministry. But it is essential that one individual act in one capacity only in any one liturgy. To have the same person proclaim the word and minister communion at the same Mass violates both the spirit and intent of paragraph 28 of the *Constitution on the Sacred Liturgy,* cited above. Each person should do only his or her own portion of the liturgy — no more and no less.

The advantage of having fewer people involved is the ability to work more closely with each person to fully develop their talents. It also helps in the training process because these people will have a fuller understanding of the interrelatedness of the various ministries. Overall teaching on liturgical principles applies to everyone so that these sessions can include everyone and can be a bit more thorough. The hands-on training unique to each ministry can be done at different times.

The number of lectors needed will depend on how many Masses you have every weekend. The ideal is to have one lector for each Mass of the month. For example, we have three Masses each weekend. Thus it is preferable to have twelve lectors or even fifteen to cover the months with five weekends. That number is a luxury I have seldom had! It is helpful for your people if they are scheduled to be the lector at the Mass they normally attend. Again, this is not always possible. Our lectors are rotated as needed, taking into account their schedules for other ministries and their personal preferences.

As was mentioned earlier, ministers in small parishes usually wear many hats. The caution is to not use the same people all the time. There may be others just waiting to be asked. Just because there were only six people willing to be lectors this year doesn't mean that others may not be moved to join you next year, especially when they see that those who are involved receive good training and improve their skills over time. We need to always be on the alert for new people.

Eucharistic Ministers The 1978 document from the National Conference of Catholic Bishops entitled *This Holy and Living Sacrifice* (HLS) made provision for lay ministers of communion following the 1973 papal document *Immensae Caritatis.* This was to facilitate communion under both kinds at Sunday eucharistic celebrations when there were not enough priests and deacons, and it allowed the local bishop to appoint both men and women to this ministry.

In a small parish, lay ministers of communion are especially necessary because there is seldom more than one priest. Even when we are fortunate enough to have a deacon, extra ministers are needed for the cup. According to HLS #33, there should be two ministers of the consecrated wine for each minister of the consecrated bread. So even if only the pastor will distribute the consecrated bread and a deacon is available for the cup, at least one additional lay minister will be needed to facilitate a smooth flow of the communion rite.

The training of those entrusted with this ministry is especially important. Of all the ministries, this is the one that requires a special grace of movement and reverence of touch. In addition to the usual understanding of their role and its function within the larger picture of liturgy, these ministers must show their joy and reverence in the manner in which they carry the sacred vessels and serve. "A true reverence for what they carry is to be seen and felt by all: not a false humility, but a strong sense of joy and delight in the sharing of the Lord's body and blood. That can translate to how the plate is picked up and carried, how the minister stands, how the cup or plate is later returned to a side table. It may be as simple a matter as using both hands, rather than one, to carry the plate or cup."[9]

The selection of those who serve in this ministry must be undertaken with care. It needs the input of the pastor, and the actual invitation may best come from him. The choice is not, and must not be seen as, a reward for service to the church. In our small communities it often seems that the same group of people does everything. Sometimes this is a fact of life, given our numbers and the human tendency to be either "doers" or "watchers" (with "watchers" making up the majority). However, this is a wonderful opportunity to get some of the "watchers" involved.

Eucharistic ministers should also reflect the community as a whole, including both men and women and adults of all ages and stations. Obviously, these ministers should be practicing Catholics who are a regular part of the parish assembly. It is also a good idea to allow neophytes time to absorb the mystery of what they have become and to arrive at a good understanding of the sacrament. They may then become excellent examples to the community in the way that they bring a special sense of awe to their role in the communion rite.

In small parishes, the number of those who serve as eucharistic ministers will be small, so they must not feel like or be seen as an elite group. Their role as servants should be obvious to all. This is another reason a good formation program is essential.[10]

Ushers and Greeters This is often referred to as the ministry of hospitality. When it is a fully functional ministry, it is the first contact visitors have with your parish and can set the tone for their entire experience with you. Unfortunately, this ministry is generally not appreciated and is held in somewhat low esteem. Most ushers would be surprised to learn that theirs is a ministry defined in the *General Instruction of the Roman Missal.* In Section III, "Special Ministers," #68b and #68c specifically include "those who meet the people at the church entrance, seat them, and direct processions" and "those who take up the collection." In paragraph 70 of the same section, ushers are part of the ministries included in the group of those that may be performed by women.

The act of gathering is important. Sunday gatherings are a family reunion of sorts, and the ushers are the ones who open the door to the fellowship of that family gathered in the Lord. That need for fellowship, for a kind word of recognition and acceptance as a fellow human, is no less present in a small community than in a large one. The need for "ushering" people to their seats is usually not required in a small parish, but helping the elderly or infirm to their places may still be appreciated. Kindness and hospitality to the stranger is still accomplished by introducing them to other parishioners. A smiling face sets the tone for the worship experience to follow.

Too often, the ministry of usher is seen as limited to taking up the collection. This is an important function, but the ministry of hospitality goes much further. These ministers see to the general order of the worshiping body and are ready to assist those who may need them. In addition to greeting people, they are there to direct strangers to facilities and services and to assist anyone who needs help during the service, perhaps assisting the disabled or elderly during communion and again greeting people and handing out bulletins at the door at the close of Mass. In addition, they must remember that they also are part of the worshiping community.

This ministry has resisted any organization in my own community. The attempt to include women met with no success — they just were not comfortable in that role. But somehow the ministry does get done. There are always full-time people around to spot visitors and make them feel welcome (we are a resort parish), and there is an understood arrangement that determines who will take up the collection. This pattern has been observed in other small parishes in our area, so I assume it is not an unknown practice.

Even though this unorganized approach does accomplish the task, there is still room for improvement, which can only occur with training. Even in our parish, a more consistent approach came about after those involved received a small booklet on the ministry of ushers that gave them the history of the ministry as well as many practical suggestions (see footnote #5). Even though the women were uncomfortable taking up the collection, they took a more visible role in the hospitality aspect of the ministry after learning more about it from this book.

If you are able to build a more structured ministry, the people who are currently involved will be the best teachers and probably the best at finding and inviting others to join them. This is also a ministry our young people can share in. Often they are ill-at-ease with more visible roles but can be naturals at greeting other young people and helping them feel welcome. As with all ministries, the defined roles in any book usually require some modifications for small communities. That doesn't mean we don't fulfill the ministry; we just do it differently. When most of the assembly knows one another by name, hospitality is already a fact of life.

Altar Servers This ministry is currently in a state of change. For many years it was a ministry carried out primarily by young boys. Vested in albs or in cassocks and surplices, they carried the processional cross and candles and assisted the celebrant with the book, incense and sacred vessels, all the while trying to remain still and attentive. Prior to Vatican II, they were required to learn all the Latin responses and certain prayers. It was a time-honored tradition for young boys, some of whom continued to serve through high school. Having been an altar boy was a good recommendation in life.

Since Vatican II, this ministry has seen changes, not just in the tasks (learning Latin responses is certainly not a requirement today!) but in the level of interest in fulfilling the ministry. Today's young people are involved in so many outside activities and sports that it seems more difficult to get the commitment necessary, both from them and from their parents. Without parish schools, small parishes have a more difficult time finding candidates for this ministry.

The growing pressure for inclusivity in all ministries created additional tension for this ministry in the United States. In 1994, the long-awaited approval for girls to serve in this capacity was received. We will see additional changes as the Bishops' Committee puts forth their new guidelines for servers. Official approval for girls to serve at the altar may make it easier for the small parish to build up this ministry; it definitely increases the number of young people available to serve.

The requirements of this ministry would seem to make it questionable for the very young, although by tradition that is centuries-old, most altar servers began at a young age. Regardless of the decision in your parish regarding the age of servers, it is essential that sound training be part of the program. Without the training and drill in the requirements of this office, it can be more of a distraction during liturgy. Doing without servers is preferable to having untrained ones.

The ideal program will have at least one adult in charge of training, scheduling and assisting these young people. This coordinator must be thoroughly familiar with the duties required of this ministry and must be a good teacher. A sound program for young people in this ministry can yield great fruits in the future if it doesn't just train in the mechanics of serving but also instills an understanding of and love for good liturgy. This ministry certainly includes young people in the life of the parish, helping them realize that they too are part of the Body of Christ.

Sacristan For most of us, the sacristan is such a behind-the-scenes minister that we may not realize this ministry even exists. However, a well-trained sacristan can definitely make the life of the pastor easier. Dirty linens, spotted vestments, tarnished silver and a dusty environment do not speak well of the sacredness of our celebration. This is underscored in the *Ceremonial of Bishops,* #38: "The first of all the elements belonging to the beauty of the place where the liturgy is celebrated is the spotless condition of the floor and walls and of all the images and articles that will be used or seen during a service."

All these elements are the jurisdiction of the sacristan. This does not mean that he or she must do all of the cleaning, polishing and laundry but that the coordination of these jobs belongs to him or her. In a small parish, the task is somewhat less formidable but is no less important. The correct number of candles for each season must be ordered; sufficient altar linens must be clean and ready; the priest's and deacon's vestments, in the correct color for the season or celebration, must be clean and pressed along with those for the altar servers; there must be enough bread and wine; and everything needed for the celebration must be clean, polished and ready.

In some parishes, other people take on the responsibility of cleaning the church and sanctuary, and someone other than the sacristan may take on the task of washing and ironing altar linens. Many of the specific tasks can be delegated, thus involving more people, especially those who wish to work in less public ministries. But if one person doesn't oversee and coordinate the total process, some tasks may fall between the cracks, and something important may be missing or undone at a crucial time.[11]

This ministry is described near the end of our list, but it is an essential ministry for any smoothly functioning parish. Most parishes have someone doing most of the tasks described (or Father is doing them himself!), but there may be no formal position of sacristan. This is especially true for the small parish. If there is no one doing these things, the priest may be very happy to have the help. In finding the right person for this position, bear in mind that whoever it is will have to work very closely with him, and he may have suggestions.

On the other hand, if there is someone who has done all this for years, that person can be of great help to you. Tread softly in making suggestions or changes. If, in fact, this area is running smoothly, don't rock the boat. The person in charge here can be of great help to you in learning about the parish's history, people and operations.

Art & Environment This ministry will evolve as other ministries and liturgical planning grow. This is not to say that it isn't important; but to begin here would be putting the cart before the horse. There is decoration in every parish, even if only for special seasons. Those who perform this task usually do so because they enjoy the work. As with all ministries, coming in with a new agenda will only create tensions. As other areas of ministry are developed and put into place, the need for a more formal plan will become apparent.

There is a natural evolution in the training of people in this ministry. If you are able to expose them to larger liturgical celebrations and workshops that celebrate extensive liturgies, you won't be able to hold them back. This is one area where ideas are contagious. The difficulty will be in helping your people realize that what is appropriate in a huge space for a special liturgy may not be appropriate in a smaller space in Ordinary Time. Here again, experience is the best teacher, and this is an area where the freedom to be creative is needed.

Helping those involved to recognize the correct color for each season is a good start. It is amazing how many people think the correct colors for the Christmas season are red and green. But once the proper colors of white with gold and red accents are introduced, the results usually end any questions. Also, assisting these ministers in recognizing the degree of festivity and the nature of each season will result in worship environments that truly enhance the season.

It is also a good idea to familiarize these ministers with the liturgical calendar and the sequence of the seasons. They need to know the necessity of not introducing Christmas decor during Advent or jumping ahead into Easter during Lent and Holy Week. In one parish we visited during Advent, the Christmas trees were already up and decorated, and the nativity scene was put in place by the second week of Advent.

Once a coordinator of this ministry is identified, that person should be introduced to the document *Environment and Art in Catholic Worship* (EACW).[12] This will provide a firm basis of understanding for the place of art and decoration in the worship environment as well as an overall understanding of worship space. In addition, *Sourcebook for Sundays and Seasons* (published annually by LTP) is a valuable source of ideas.[13] It helps define the seasons and celebrations, which will give artistically inclined people a direction for their talents.

Bear in mind that this ministry, much like any other, will not come to fullness of expression or appropriateness overnight. By allowing it to blossom at its own pace, those involved will grow in their appreciation of the liturgy and their role in it. When this ministry comes into its own, it is a thing of beauty indeed (no pun intended!).

Lay Presiders This is a ministry of special importance for small parishes because we frequently find ourselves in the position of having no ordained minister available at a time when public prayer is needed. While we all know that praying is not the special province of the ordained and is something we all do every day, leading public prayer is another matter entirely. And it is not something that comes easily to most of us. However, it is something for which we can prepare ourselves.

When is this likely to be an issue in our parishes? Most of us are accustomed to having daily Mass, but what if our pastor is not available every day? How do we handle a wake service if the pastor is away or otherwise occupied? On a simpler level, who leads us in prayer at meetings? In recent years, the luxury of every parish having at least one full-time pastor has become just that — a luxury. Even many large parishes that used to have several associate pastors now find themselves with only one associate or none at all. The long-discussed shortage of priests is a reality, and it is changing the way we function.

The Liturgy of the Hours has assumed lay leadership to be normal for some time. Prayer formulas are given for both ordained and non-ordained leadership. This form of prayer is becoming more and more common in small groups and in parish settings. The new *Order of Christian Funerals* also takes into consideration the fact that lay people will increasingly be asked to lead portions of the rituals surrounding the actual funeral Mass. Not only is this allowed, it is encouraged as part of a parish's bereavement ministry.

The *Order of Christian Funerals,* study edition, is an excellent resource in preparing for funeral liturgies, whether led by a lay person or not.[14] The normal order of things for funeral rites now assumes lay leadership for many of the preliminary prayer services. What an opportunity for all of us! The new rituals have very specific and appropriate prayers for all the events leading up to and following the death of anyone. It allows each of us to minister in a meaningful way to our brothers and sisters at a time when words often fail us.

However, having these resources available and being able to use them are two different issues. If you have ever been asked on the spur of the moment to lead a prayer, you probably know the meaning of terror. And even if you know ahead of time, the actual moment causes a sense of panic unlike any other found in public speaking. We know we are acting out the sacred at these moments, and the importance of "doing it right" takes on different proportions. Going totally blank is not an uncommon experience.

The first time I was asked to lead a service, I spent several hours preparing, marking my pages and reading and rereading the prayers. When the time came, my knees were shaking so hard I thought everyone could surely see it! Calling on the Holy Spirit to keep me from falling over, I made it through the liturgy of the word. I managed the necessary prayers and gestures and thought I was just about home free. But when we started the Lord's Prayer, I went completely blank! It might as well have been the chemical formula for rocket fuel. After that, I clipped a copy of it in my book. No matter how well you know something, when you have to lead, the memory is not the most reliable of tools. It was after that experience that I understood why the presider uses the sacramentary for every part of the Mass!

There are some liturgical aspects of leading prayer that we don't usually have to consider in our planning. Lay leaders need practical information such as where to sit (not in the celebrant's chair), what to wear, where to stand and how to gesture, and which forms of greetings and blessings lay presiders are to use. It is important not to clericalize this role. We have a legitimate role as presiders at specific times, and there is no need to pretend to be something we are not or to appear to be other than lay people. Doing so only confuses people. If we want to be taken seriously in the role of presider, it must be apparent that we are part of the assembly exercising a specific role and are not above or more important than the assembly.

It takes time and practice to be able to lead prayer, and for some it will never be less than an ordeal. As with all ministries, not everyone is called to or able to fulfill this role. In fairness to both minister and people, this ministry needs the appropriate training.[15]

Looking to the Future

Sunday Worship in the Absence of a Priest (SWAP) is now a reality rather than a possibility. In 1991, the Bishops' Committee on the Liturgy published its statement on this issue, *Gathered in Steadfast Faith,* to coincide with the publication of the ritual book *Sunday Celebrations in the Absence of a Priest.* This document provides guidance on this subject, from the selection and training of those who will lead and their commissioning to the principles and structure of these celebrations. It also emphasizes the tradition and preeminence of Sunday as the Lord's Day.

For many small parishes, SWAP has been a reality for some time. How do we function in the absence of a full-time pastor or with no pastor? Many parishes are run by lay administrators and pastoral assistants. How do we continue to be a parish and meet the sacramental needs of our communities, especially the need for eucharist?

This is an issue that raises many questions for which there are few answers. As a sacramental people, we recognize that the eucharist is central to our worship. But a communion service is not eucharist. This difference is not lost on priests, deacons, liturgists and catechists but usually is lost on the average parishioner.

At both celebrations, people understand that they are receiving communion. We have spent the years since Vatican II trying to educate people that eucharist is something we do together — priest and people — not something that is done to or for us. What does it say, then, when we have a priest come by periodically and consecrate enough bread to last until he comes again? In the long run, will this stopgap measure of using lay presiders to lead communion services on Sunday help us or harm us?

James Dallen, a well-known priest, teacher and author, has taken up this subject in his book *The Dilemma of Priestless Sundays.* In it, he discusses the impact of these lay-led celebrations on our Catholic spirituality.[16] If we substitute the liturgy of the word and the distribution of communion for the communal celebration of the eucharist, are we in danger of losing an essential ingredient in our Catholic spirituality? It is an issue that will shape our spiritual futures dramatically.

Kathleen Hughes, RSCJ, professor of liturgy at Catholic Theological Union in Chicago, has also discussed this topic and some of the questions raised by it. How will it change the role of the ordained priesthood, and how will it change the role of lay leaders? Is there the same tie of obedience and accountability to the bishop by lay leaders as by priests? What training and education is going to be available to and required of these lay leaders? After raising people's understanding of and desire for the eucharist on a regular, even daily, basis, it will be very difficult to change.

We as liturgists will be dealing with this issue for some time. I fear that the idea of priestless communion services may be a liturgical Band-Aid for a much deeper ecclesial wound. If we respect our traditions and each other, there is hope that we will find a cure for the wound, and it will leave us stronger as a people of God.

In summary, when we speak of the priesthood of all believers, it would be good to remember Paul's teachings on unity. In his First Letter to the Corinthians he reminds us that the Body of Christ is like our own individual bodies — many different parts making up only one body. Just as our feet have a distinct characteristic and function, they do not fulfill that function except as part of our entire body. Eucharistic ministers also have a distinct function, but they also are not able to fulfill that function except as part of the Body of Christ. Paul tells us that there are many gifts given but that all are for the good of the Body. Within our parish communities we have many gifts, many ministries, but none of them is independent of the whole. If the Body of Christ is to be healthy, we must tend to the needs of each member of the Body, working together, assisting the weaker members and developing the strengths of all as we strive to glorify that Body for the kingdom of God.

●

1 General Instruction of the Roman Missal, #58.

2 Constitution on the Sacred Liturgy, #14.

3 Introduction to the General Instruction of the Roman Missal, *#5.*

4 General Instruction of the Roman Missal, *#70.*

5 In its Ministry Series, The Liturgical Press offers several short volumes on the various ministries: The Ministry of the Cantor, The Ministry of Musicians, The Ministry of Communion, The Liturgical Ministry of Deacons, The Ministry to Persons with Disabilities, The Ministry of Hospitality, The Ministry of the Sacristan: Preparing and Maintaining the Liturgical Space, The Ministry of Servers, The Ministry of Ushers.

6 Introduction to the Constitution on the Sacred Liturgy, *#28.*

7 Two videos on the ministry of the lector are available: Proclaiming the Word: Formation for Readers in the Liturgy *(Chicago: Liturgy Training Publications, 1994), and* The Word of the Lord *(Chicago: Liturgy Training Publications, 1995).*

8 Workbook for Lectors and Gospel Readers *(Chicago: Liturgy Training Publications), annually.*

9 Gabe Huck, Liturgy with Style and Grace, *2nd ed. (Chicago: Liturgy Training Publications, 1984), 59.*

10 An excellent source for all ministers is Joseph M. Champlin, An Important Office of Immense Love *(Ramsey, NJ: Paulist Press, 1980). This book gives the minister both the history and practical concerns of the ministry and deals with the inner or spiritual qualities of the minister. It also gives practical suggestions for beginning this program in your parish.*

11 An excellent resource for the sacristan, both for training and for reference, is G. Thomas Ryan, The Sacristy Manual *(Chicago: Liturgy Training Publications, 1993). This book should be available in all sacristies to assist those who perform this important ministry. The everyday tasks are fairly easy to remember, but many things are done only once a year, such as Holy Week and Triduum, and others only occasionally, such as weddings, funerals and the Bishop's visits. Each has special requirements, and no one can remember everything.*

12 See National Conference of Catholic Bishops, Environment & Art in Catholic Worship *(Chicago: Liturgy Training Publications, 1993).*

13 This is an annual publication from Liturgy Training Publications.

14 From Liturgy Training Publications, 1990.

15 A helpful book in this regard is Kathleen Hughes, RSCJ, Lay Presiding: The Art of Leading Prayer *(Collegeville, MN: The Liturgical Press, 1988). It not only gives guidelines for gesture and presence but also basic formulas for the composition of original prayers. This is an excellent resource to assist those called upon to lead prayer for meetings or small groups. However, anyone who is going to lead larger services really needs to work with the pastor or with a diocesan training program.*

16 James Dallen, The Dilemma of Priestless Sundays *(Chicago: Liturgy Training Publications, 1994).*

CHAPTER 5

Sing a Joyful Song

What Should We Sing?

"Among the many signs and symbols used by the church to celebrate its faith, music is of preeminent importance. As sacred song united to words, it forms a necessary or integral part of the solemn liturgy."[1] The language of the documents leaves little question as to the role of music in liturgical celebration. The question of whether to have music or not is not open to debate. Sung liturgies are the norm.

As with all norms, small parishes need to be more creative in fulfilling this requirement. Most of us just don't have the resources, either in money or in talent, to mount large-scale music programs. Such programs are not necessary to fulfill the need for music. As with other aspects of the liturgy, the assembly is the primary source of music and its participation is foremost in importance.

It is important to distinguish that we are not talking about *singing at liturgy* but rather *sung liturgy.* This is a departure from the old four-hymn model of Mass in which singing was an added but not integral part of the celebration. This model was developed within the context of the Latin Mass; vernacular singing only fit at specific points. But even though now the entire Mass is in the vernacular, we often continue to embrace the four-hymn style. It is past time to reevaluate the place of music in our celebrations in light of the liturgical renewal of Vatican II.

Music in Catholic Worship (#54) and *Liturgical Music Today* (#17) state very clearly and specifically that the most important elements of sung prayer are the acclamations, which ought to be sung even at Masses where little else is sung. These acclamations are the Alleluia; Holy, Holy, Holy; Memorial Acclamation and Great Amen; and the doxology to the Lord's Prayer. There are numerous musical settings for these acclamations, many of which are suitable for unaccompanied voices. Almost everyone knows an old chant version or can pick one up quickly. (Chanting seems to be in our genes as Catholics.)

With the exception of the Embolism to the Lord's Prayer, these acclamations belong to the people even though they may be led by the presider, cantor or choir. Additionally, if your pastor is especially musical, there are now several settings of the eucharistic prayers that have all or portions of the prayer sung by the presider. They also include not only the standard acclamations but additional acclamations throughout the prayer, making it a unified action or prayer of the entire community.

The responsorial psalm is another important song. By their very nature, psalms are meant to be sung. The word "psalm" means song. If you read through the texts of the scriptures, you will find that most of the psalms have a definite meter. Singing the responsorial psalm doesn't require a professional musician, although some musical ability is needed. There are excellent sources of chant settings for the psalms that are effective and easy for both leader and assembly. For example, Oregon Catholic Press publishes *Respond and Acclaim* as part of its parish music program. It contains simple chant settings for both the weekly psalm and the gospel acclamation. Size, or lack of it, is no reason not to sing or chant the psalm.

The two processional chants or songs deemed important are the entrance or gathering song and the communion song. Both create and remind us of our unity. They can be hymns, songs or chants. Many of the same chants used as responsorial psalms are quite appropriate here, and because of their ease and familiarity can be very conducive to assembly participation. During communion, a simple chant or tune that is also musically and scripturally appropriate is more likely to result in participation. People are not going to carry books to communion, despite the desires of many liturgical musicians.

When we start discussing music in parish planning meetings, we can get into real problems. Not everyone, of course, has the same taste in music. When music is chosen for liturgy, it is important to have someone who has a sensitivity to the tastes and abilities of the community as well as musical skill help make the decisions. The best piece of music will not assist prayer if it is too difficult to sing. But don't underestimate the assembly. We don't need to sing "Home on the Range" to enable the assembly's voice! There are so many styles of church music available today — from traditional hymns to folk and contemporary music — that the musical repertoire of a parish can have something for everyone.

This doesn't mean that you will be able to please everyone. But if the music chosen supports the scriptures and the ritual action of the Mass, the quality of worship is greatly enhanced. Since we generally have a limited number of musicians in small parishes, it may be necessary to concentrate most of our efforts on one specific Mass every week. But if it is possible, singing the acclamations should be standard for every Mass.

The most important asset to a music program is an accompanist, either on organ or piano. If your parish can afford nothing else to enhance its liturgy, this is where your limited dollars ought to go. You may have a very talented singer to lead your people, able choir members and an assembly with a real desire to sing, but without support from piano or organ, your music program will be limited. One or two guitars would be very helpful in the absence of a keyboard accompanist, and if this is what you have, go with it and grow with it. But this means that those guitarists should be able to play more than just basic chords and be willing to learn.

This is not to put down guitars as suitable accompaniment, but there is a limit to how well one can teach music without a keyboard. There are some pieces of music that need a guitar and cannot be done effectively without one, and it is quite possible to have a vigorous music program with good guitar accompaniment. But keep looking for a keyboard player. This doesn't mean someone who is just learning or who really can't play well — it is too important a position. Obviously, you take what you have and work from there, but using someone who is not musically literate or capable as an accompanist can do more harm than good. If someone is willing to volunteer, that's wonderful — but this is a position that requires many years of training, and Christian justice demands a willingness to pay for that training and ability. You may find someone in the music department of a nearby school, or you may be able to share an accompanist with another church in town if your schedules permit. Because the order of worship is not the same in all churches and some components of the Roman Catholic Mass may be unfamiliar, the accompanist may need liturgical guidance to become familiar with our Mass structure.

Unaccompanied or *a capella* singing is also a wonderful exercise for your assembly if you have someone who can lead. It is good on occasion, but for worship week in and week out, some instrumental support is necessary. We like to use unaccompanied assembly singing for specific settings, such as during Lent or Advent. One good example is a chanted setting of a psalm. Pieces from the Taizé community in France, which are very simple and effective repetitive refrains, are also good. We regularly use "Jesus, Remember Me" during the veneration of the cross on Good Friday and "Stay With Me" at other times during the Triduum.[2] Taizé also has many pieces, especially Latin refrains, which will please your older members!

The Iona Community in Scotland has several simple unaccompanied pieces.[3] We discovered the value of preparing the assembly for unaccompanied singing when our organist was gone for two months one summer. We planned our summer liturgies with this in mind. While this should not be the norm, it was a wonderful experience that resulted in an unexpected increase in the participation of our assembly. The better participation continued even when our organist returned. It was almost as if they had found their voices and realized they really could sing!

Creating Musical Ritual

If there is limited music or none at all in your parish, be aware that it will take some time to develop a repertoire that your community is comfortable singing. Most musicians want variety, but repetition is at the heart of ritual, liturgical or otherwise. The same acclamations need to be done until they become part of the people's prayer. We have spent six years building a selection of acclamations that our people know. Now we are able to identify each season with a specific set of acclamations used only during that season. Just as hearing "Silent Night" immediately identifies Christmas, the acclamations from "Mass of Remembrance" signal the beginning of Lent for our parish.[4] Now our people can pray the acclamations and not just sing them, because they know them by heart. This takes time to accomplish, but the results are worth the wait.

The choice of music is not something to be taken lightly. It is an integral part of the Mass. The liturgy documents and all the commentaries on them emphasize the importance of sound pastoral judgment. There are many popular songs that people think would be nice to use at liturgy, but "nice" is not a criterion. Neither is the phrase we hear too often in planning diocesan liturgies: "Let's sing something everybody knows." In the first place, there is no such animal; and second, a piece of music must reflect, support and enhance the ritual action taking place. "Enhance" here does not mean beautifying but rather adding aural substance and meaning to a symbol or ritual. A gathering song that speaks of coming together and a communion song that speaks of the bread and wine are examples of music that enhances the ritual.

In assessing music, the first judgment is musical. Is it technically well-written? Is it singable by most people, or does the range go so high that only a soprano can reach the notes? Is it aesthetically pleasing — does it sound good? Even if it passes these criteria, it still may not be suitable. Many popular and show tunes are musically sound (or they wouldn't be popular) but lack liturgical and pastoral qualities.

Music needs to enrich the liturgy, not detract from it. What you choose should be ritually appropriate, both in content and in style and for those who are singing. For example, a long gathering song followed by a lengthy, sung "Lord have mercy" and a complicated "Glory to God" may make the liturgy of the word seem insignificant. Using a full musical setting of a psalm that takes five or six minutes when the readings are thirty seconds long is unproportional and becomes performance-oriented. Loading all the music at the beginning of Mass and then speaking the acclamations makes the eucharistic actions seem less important.

The music selected also needs to reflect the season and the degree of solemnity of the celebration. What is appropriate for Easter Sunday is overpowering on the Twenty-third Sunday in Ordinary Time. Conversely, the simple liturgy that is adequate for the Fourteenth Sunday in Ordinary Time doesn't have the degree of festivity and celebration required of a major feast day like Christmas.

The relationship of musical texts to specific scriptures is also important. Does the music under consideration help make the day's readings more meaningful? By choosing music that enhances the scriptures, the musicians can give more meaning to the message of God's word. This selection process requires analyzing the *entire text* of a piece of music. Just because "water" is in a song does not mean that it will be appropriate for baptism or for the Easter Vigil. A particular verse might best be dropped if it doesn't fit. Often I find that words I have heard hundreds of times have a new impact when they are set to good music. Singing the words we have just heard proclaimed or hearing the words proclaimed that we have just sung reinforces the message.

The placement of the music within the liturgy is also important. Singing about preparing to receive the Lord in the eucharist as a closing song doesn't make sense. Today there is a wide enough variety of music available that it is easy to choose music that says something about coming together as family or church for gathering or that has a eucharistic tone for communion. The problem isn't finding enough music — it's limiting the choices so that the assembly is not constantly learning new music.

There is also a pastoral judgment concerning music, although it can be argued that everything just discussed is pastoral. But more specifically, it is important to know the people and to be sensitive to the culture, age, social circumstances and level of faith of the community gathered to worship. Music is an important sign and symbol, and this awareness needs to be part of the planning process.

"The quality of joy and enthusiasm which music adds to community worship cannot be gained in any other way."[5] The quality of our community's sung prayer rests with the music ministers of our parish. They must be an integral part of the planning process.

Another significant part of your music program is its resources. Which is the better choice for your community — a hard-cover hymnal, a soft-cover annual music book plus missalette, or a weekly or seasonal worship aid? Look at what has been used or is available, and look at the costs involved. There are many resources to choose from, and each has its own advantages. It is necessary to find the right program for your particular situation. Talk to other liturgists and music directors to see what has worked for them. Take the time to choose wisely, and then stick with it. Give your good choice time to work. Remember that any change takes time before people become familiar and comfortable with it.

Who Will Lead Them?

Learning music and participating in sung prayer doesn't happen overnight for most assemblies. It takes leadership. This is a situation in which choirs can't but cantors can. The importance of the choir is another issue, and this discussion is not meant to take away from their place in worship. However, a well-trained cantor can help overcome the reluctance to sing found in some assemblies.

"While there is no place in the liturgy for display of virtuosity for its own sake, artistry is valued, and an individual singer can effectively lead the assembly, attractively proclaim the word of God in the psalm . . . and take his or her part in other responsorial singing. . . . The presence of such a singer is desirable even in churches which have a choir."[6] Even in the smallest parish, there is usually at least one person who sings well. The ministry does not require an operatic voice. In fact, that would be a distraction. It does, however, require a certain amount of musical ability and the ability to lead people, welcome them and make them feel comfortable in their own musical role. The cantor should not dominate the singing but rather animate the assembly's song. This is a confidence which can be built by training, practice and experience. The same is true of the "technical" skills necessary. The cantor must know the sound system and be comfortable using a microphone. As the assembly's leader of song, the cantor should sing with the people, not add a harmony. And there must be recognition of the cantor's role as minister or servant rather than performer. They are leaders of sung prayer.

Many parishes have someone who plays the guitar and leads the singing. Others have an organist or pianist who also leads the singing. This is obviously better than no leader at all and may be the best place to start in your parish. Some hand movement is necessary to be an effective leader, yet in this situation, hand gestures are difficult at best. It is also important that the cantor be seen by the assembly. A disembodied voice is not much incentive to sing.

Training for cantors is available from various sources. The Ministry Series mentioned earlier includes a booklet by James Hansen, one of the leading teachers on this subject, that gives both background and practical suggestions for the cantor.[7] Liturgy Training Publications has three video programs and a book to help cantors and singers.[8] Hearing and seeing good examples is always more effective than reading about how to do it and is helpful to those who are unable to attend "live" training sessions.

An excellent program is also available each summer from the National Association of Pastoral Musicians (NPM). This is an association of church musicians who have joined together for the purpose of developing and supporting good liturgical music; it includes musicians from all over the country. It is for composers, directors, cantors, teachers and singers interested in liturgical music. They conduct an intensive, week-long program that covers theology and scripture as well as vocal technique. It is held in various locations every year during the summer. For anyone with the time and the funds, this is a good opportunity. Your diocesan office of worship may also sponsor cantor workshops from time to time. If not, suggest it.

A good cantor program can be the building block for a parish music program. As the cantors and assembly get to know one another in this liturgical role, a rapport and sense of trust is built. The assembly can be comfortable singing because there is someone to let them know when to sing and to give them a voice to follow. A parish can do without a cantor for every liturgy if the resources aren't available, but for major feasts it is a practical necessity; these liturgies have additional components—many of them musical—and a cantor can keep things flowing smoothly.

Choirs Have Many Styles

"A well-trained choir adds beauty and solemnity to the liturgy and also assists and encourages the singing of the congregation."[9] The liturgy documents make it clear that the establishment of a choir, even a small one, is important to the liturgical life of a parish. This is one area where most resources are of very little help. They are geared toward the traditional choir that does four-part harmony and has more members than we usually have assembled for Mass! A choir is simply more than one or two people who rehearse and sing together, both in a leadership role and in meditation music. More properly referred to as a schola, this small group can be very effective in adding a musical dimension to liturgical celebrations.

Our choir has ranged from an all-time high of fourteen members to a summer low of three members, including the organist! Our average over the past six years has been eight. With this number we have done various styles of music from four-part harmony to simple, unison, *a capella* pieces. Our choir includes our three cantors, which gives us three strong voices for harmony. But this development took time. We started with unison music that we could do well. There is nothing like success to encourage people. During those periods when our numbers are low, the choir does fewer pieces by itself but has specific pieces that work very well with as few as three voices. Many of these are Taizé or Iona Community pieces (as mentioned earlier), but most of the unison pieces from our hymnal work well, too. Some of these may be very appropriate for a specific liturgy but do not warrant the time and effort to add them to the assembly's inventory of music. Before we teach the assembly a new piece of music, the choir will use it alone and a reduced choir of two or three works well for this task.

Having a choir, however small, adds to the sense of celebration. It also assists the assembly in learning new music. It is easier to learn something if you can hear others singing with confidence. The choir also is support for the cantor — at least they will sing when the assembly is not participating well! How small is too small? The presence of Christ is found "where two or three are gathered . . .", and that includes choirs.

A word here about the reason for a choir's existence. The primary purpose of a choir is to lead and augment the singing of the assembly. Yes, there are roles that the choir fills by singing without the assembly, but that music must still add to or amplify ritual or scripture and not merely be a performance of musical skills. Using an ornate piece of baroque Latin music as a gathering song not only robs the assembly of its rightful role but does not serve to unite the people into a worshiping body, as a gathering song should. It may take some time to reorient your choir to a leadership role if their history has been one of "performing" music for the glory of God.

While repetition is necessary for good ritual, it can get boring for your choir. Because musicians crave more complex and challenging music, having one or two concerts a year is a good solution. This allows your musicians to exhibit skills of which they are justifiably proud and can serve as a good recruiting and training tool. We also do a half-hour concert prior to the Christmas Vigil Mass, and we have created a liturgy that incorporates scripture readings, community carols and more elaborate choir music. Since we use traditional carols during the Christmas season, we are able to use our rehearsal time to prepare some very challenging music for this occasion.

How important is it to have music be part of your celebrations? Next to having the word proclaimed well, it is the most essential lay ministry. Being nourished by the word of God and the Body of Christ is the heart of our liturgies. Music is the soul. In our secular world, music expresses our joys and sorrows and mirrors our moods, and even sells everything from television shows to hamburgers. It is an important part of our culture. Can it be any less in our spiritual lives?

One lament I've often heard from people who are the sole musician and/or liturgist in a parish is that they don't have any musicians for a choir. To them and to you, I say, "broaden your horizons and lower your expectations." A person doesn't have to be able to read music and audition in our circumstances. Sometimes a truly awful voice will turn up, but most of the time, if music is chosen well, people can learn it. Most people read music to some degree — if the note goes up, it is higher; if it goes down, it is lower. The rest, such as note values and rhythm, will be learned by doing. People are often too intimidated to volunteer for the choir, thinking they need to be "good singers." Good singers are created more often than they are born.

By broadening your horizons, I mean that you should not overlook any obvious sources of music. If you have a school in your town, chances are it has some type of music program. Most high schools and many elementary schools have a choir program. Children and adults do mix for a church choir, and children grow up — two of our current members started singing with us in grade school. The younger one was almost a mascot. She is now in junior high, and her sister is a senior in high school. Both are vocal assets to our group. Young people can be effective building blocks for a parish music program, and you sometimes have to "grow your own," so to speak. It is important to take people where they are and grow with them. My parish's choir obviously is not world-renowned but in all honesty sounds better than many large choirs I have heard.

Rather than seeing what you don't have, use what you do have to its best advantage. Patience and wise choices for music will pay off. It is always difficult, and frequently impossible, to make a music program fit the usual pattern found in larger churches. But you also may find that smaller numbers and closer camaraderie results in a more committed group of musicians. We have tailored our rehearsal schedule to our members. Instead of a rigid midweek schedule, we rehearse on Sunday for the hour preceding Mass. Our members know that a midweek rehearsal won't be called unless necessary; so when one is called, they are there. Whether two or ten, the choir enjoys singing together and praising God in song.

One final word about music. It isn't the "job" of the cantor or choir to make people sing. These are ministries that enrich and enhance parish liturgies. Done well, the music ministry provides the encouragement for the assembly to find its voice so that together, you can "make a joyful noise unto the Lord."

●

1 Music in Catholic Worship, #23.

2 Jacques Berthier, "Jesus, Remember Me" and "Stay With Me" (Chicago: GIA Publications, 1981).

3 *Available through GIA Publications in Chicago.*

4 *Marty Haugen, "Mass of Remembrance," a setting of the Fourth Eucharistic Prayer of Reconciliation (Chicago: GIA Publications, 1988).*

5 Music in Catholic Worship, *#23.*

6 Music in Catholic Worship, *#35.*

7 *See note 5, chapter 4. See also Alice Parker,* Melodious Accord: Good Singing in Church *(Chicago: Liturgy Training Publications, 1991); Gabe Huck,* How Can I Keep From Singing? Thoughts about Liturgy for Musicians *(Chicago: Liturgy Training Publications, 1989).*

8 The Reason Why We Sing: Community Song with Alice Parker *(Chicago: Liturgy Training Publications, 1995);* When We Sing: Conversations with Alice Parker and Friends *(Chicago: Liturgy Training Publications, 1994);* Yes, We'll Gather: Singing Hymns with Alice Parker *(Chicago: Liturgy Training Publications, 1993).*

9 Music in Catholic Worship, *#36.*

CHAPTER 6

Now Let's Celebrate

Many Parts, One Whole

Now that we have discussed the whats and whys of liturgy and the ministries necessary, let's talk about putting it all together. How do we take all the pieces that go into a liturgical celebration and bring them together in a cohesive manner?

Someone in a workshop once said that preparing liturgy is like stringing beads together. You pick out a gathering song, add a penitential rite and a Gloria, find a setting for the psalm to go between the readings, choose a song for the preparation of the gifts and altar and a set of acclamations, select the communion song and the closing song, and there you have a Mass. But while that's more or less true, the trick is to have each of the parts relate to the whole so that the liturgy flows smoothly from beginning to end.

Preparing the liturgy doesn't mean picking a theme and making everything fit. Every Mass has a theme already — the dying and rising of Jesus Christ. In addition, through the readings and prayers there is a direction already set forth that will make the dying and rising of Jesus Christ come alive in this time and in this place. By studying the readings and looking at the antiphons and prayers in the sacramentary, this direction usually becomes clear, which makes music selection and ideas about environment much easier.

A word of caution, however. Look for more than the surface idea. For example, at one celebration of the Baptism of the Lord, every piece of music had the word "water" in it. This misses the point. Certainly at least one piece of music related to baptism is in order, but what of the other messages, such as the revelation of Jesus as the Son of God and servant of God, or the message of God's love for us? In order to open up readings for our assemblies, we need to look at the whole picture in the planning process.

Each part of the Mass must relate to the others if the liturgy as a whole is to have continuity. If the music has nothing to do with the readings, it just fills time. If the environment doesn't speak of the season, why is it there? Looking pretty and sounding pretty isn't enough of a reason to be a part of the liturgy.

The difference in really preparing liturgy, not just plugging in some music and adding a few flowers, is similar to preparing a meal. Opening a can of soup will feed your body, but preparing a meal with attention to the table setting, the menu and the surroundings can nourish not only the body but also the soul. The more festive the occasion, the more planning goes into the dinner. Just as opening a can of soup is sometimes the best approach to eating a meal and pulling out all the stops with your best china and silver, fresh flowers and a detailed menu is appropriate at other times, not all liturgies need the same degree of festivity and preparation. But they always need thought and care in the planning process. Even a soup supper can show care for those being served — dishes rather than paper plates, a warm loaf of bread and the time to enjoy each other's company.

Sometimes our liturgies tend to resemble a potluck dinner. Done well, this can be a good experience. Done poorly, some people are fed and others leave hungry. This potluck style of liturgy is frequently found in multi-cultural parishes. How do you include something for everyone? Each culture has its own beauty and spirit to add to the life of a parish, and this can be, and should be, reflected in the liturgies.

In large parishes, separate Masses in different languages are what frequently occur, creating problems when it comes to joint celebrations such as Triduum. Since we don't usually have the luxury of several Masses at a small parish, we must find other ways to be sure everyone is included. Music can provide one means of letting everyone participate in their own language. Another option for music is to use pieces such as those from the Taizé Community that have refrains in Latin. Since no one speaks Latin, everyone is on equal footing. Worship aids with the readings and other important spoken parts of the Mass printed in the second and even third language are another option.

We are primarily an Anglo parish, but because we live in an area with a large Hispanic population we sometimes have large numbers of Hispanic visitors. One option that works well is to have the Lord's Prayer and any other spoken response said in each person's own tongue. I first witnessed this at a National Association of Pastoral Musicians convention. We used Taizé music for evening prayer, and everyone was invited to pray and respond in whatever language was comfortable. Instead of a tower of Babel, we found that a warm blending of our diversity was actually a strength.

This type of "potluck" liturgy actually takes more preparation to do and to do well than first meets the eye. Otherwise it becomes very disjointed. Another type of disjointed liturgy happens when different people are in charge of different parts of the Mass but do not communicate or cooperate with one another. Even though the liturgy has a liturgy of the word and a liturgy of the eucharist, each with several different rites within them, the liturgy cannot be divided up and assigned to different people unless there is a provision for working together; everyone needs to be on the same wavelength. Communication and cooperation among ministries can make the difference between good liturgy and liturgy that just happens.

The Planning Process

The planning process tends to look different in small parishes due largely to smaller numbers and sometimes to a more relaxed style. But the question is still, "Who plans?" According to Mike Molina, director of pastoral liturgy formation for the archdiocese of Los Angeles, there are three basic models for liturgy planning. Though there are as many styles of liturgy planning as there are parishes, they usually are some form or combination of these three basic models.

The first model is the "expert" model. In a small parish, this is a good way to start. The planners include the pastor, the liturgy director, the music director, the sacristan (if you have one) and any others with liturgical education. If you have a deacon, he is also part of this model. Sometimes this model is two-tiered, with an expert group that plans and a team that carries out the details of the plan.

The second model is the "parish representative" model. This includes the "experts" plus representatives from religious education, various age groups such as the senior citizen and youth groups, the parish council, and other parish representatives. This gives the perspectives of the people in the pews but can be unwieldy. It can also waste a lot of time, since most of these representatives have little understanding of the liturgical process. They are, however, an excellent group for evaluation of liturgical practices.

The third model is the "liturgical ministries" model. This includes the core group of experts plus the coordinator of each ministry, the choir director, the religious education director, the head of the RCIA and perhaps a representative from any ethnic groups in the parish. This model requires good communication but also needs more education in liturgical practices for its members.

Each of these models presumes a formal planning style. In most small parishes the planning process is more informal, and different combinations of these models are used at various times. Planning for less than a hundred families requires far less in logistics and coordination. If you only have one candidate for baptism at the Easter Vigil, there are far fewer people involved than if you are receiving 25 people. Our problem is usually finding enough people!

Each person and each parish will develop its own style of planning. How? By trial and error, and learning what works. In my own experience, a variation on each of the three models has been used at one time or another. The only thing they have had in common was that a small group did the actual planning and another group joined them for the preparation. There are many people who can help with art and environment, for example, if they are told what needs to be done. They need direction, but they love doing the work. There are people who are very artistic with flowers, but they don't know the necessary colors or placement for specific liturgies. Given a basic plan, they create real beauty.

In one of our more successful planning arrangements, the pastor and music director were able to coordinate their efforts so that the music, readings and homily were all complementary. The pastor, another liturgist and myself looked at specific rituals, usually by season, and planned such specifics as processions, art and environment, and special rites. When the deacon was part of those rituals, he was part of the planning. Coordinating the people needed, including the ministers, and putting together any needed paperwork such as a presider's book or worship aid was my job; the other liturgist coordinated the art and environment and the needs of the sacristan. The music director took care of coordinating with the organist and choir director. We only met formally five or six times a year, but since we saw each other every week, it worked. Our formal meetings tended to be vision and evaluation sessions, looking at what direction we wanted to go in and what changes had to be made.

Speaking of changes, unless you live in an area where weather is never a problem and everyone always shows up when they say they will, you need to build a backup plan into major liturgies. No matter how far in advance you plan or how much detail goes into the process, there are always "circumstances beyond our control," as the saying goes. For a Sunday liturgy, most absences can be covered at the last minute; but if a blizzard arrives during Holy Week (and I have had it happen), all plans go out the window. So it is always a good idea to have a Plan B.

Among the liturgists I know, we each have our own approach to the planning process. And all of us have experienced the need to adapt that approach with a change of pastors. Each pastor has his own style of collaborating with his staff, and while some will adapt to the process in place, most of the time a new pastor means a new direction. And a new direction usually means growth. Build on what you have, and be open to new ways of thinking and doing. While the principles remain the same, the practice has as many variations as there are parishes. Change can be painful, but to quote a line from the movie *Teahouse of the August Moon,* "Pain makes us think, thought makes us wise, and wisdom makes life endurable."

The Cycle of Life

One additional area that needs to be considered in the planning process is the liturgical calendar, or cycle of seasons. This cycle of seasons is the way we as church experience the paschal mystery of Christ in our lives. "Christ's saving work is celebrated in sacred memory by the church on fixed days throughout the year. Each week on the day called the Lord's Day, the church commemorates the Lord's resurrection. Once a year at Easter the church honors this resurrection and passion with the utmost solemnity. In fact, through the yearly cycle, the church unfolds the entire mystery of Christ and keeps the anniversaries of the saints."[1]

It is through our prayers and celebrations, especially our celebration of the eucharist, that we make each day holy. The document *General Norms for the Liturgical Year and the Calendar* sets the seasons, feasts, memorials and solemnities. Because each has its own character, we must know that character and its requirements if we are to prepare the appropriate rites for its celebration. The seasons around Christmas and Easter, for instance, have many special rites and rules. We may think we know them, but because of their infrequent nature, an examination of the *General Instruction of the Roman Missal,* the sacramentary itself and any other resources is not only helpful but necessary.

The seasons and cycles provide part of the catechetical nature of our liturgy. They are the means by which our formation and education take place. We use these special days and seasons to celebrate the life of Christ from his incarnation and birth through his passion, resurrection and ascension. We learn his teachings and what is expected of us as his followers. The history of our church from the coming of the Holy Spirit at Pentecost to the early churches of Corinth, Ephesus and Rome are celebrated and explained as we go through the church year.

For those of us in small parishes, these seasons can really be used as a teaching tool, reaching perhaps a larger percentage of our parishioners than would occur in a large parish. The special liturgies, such as those for the Triduum, usually require a larger number of people both for the preparations and for the actual liturgy. At a recent Holy Thursday liturgy, we had 17 people plus our pastor and deacon in the procession. Not counting our choir, that was almost 30% of the assembly! Because we are small, such things usually do involve a high percentage of our people.

Because some rehearsal was needed for that procession, it was an opportunity for catechesis. The participants heard about the history and meaning of the Triduum and why it is so important in the church year and in their lives. A teacher of mine once said that if you talk to ten people about something, you actually reach about 40 because each person tells at least three others! Through such small gatherings, we are able to use the special seasons to help our people develop a better understanding of our history and of the spirituality of Christian life.

Another aspect of these cycles is that they help people see that the liturgical cycle is not so much a circle as a spiral. How have we grown as individuals and as a parish from one Advent season to the next? Our liturgies for each season are repetitive from one year to the next, but through homilies, discussion groups and handout materials, we build on the experiences of previous years.[2]

The other part of the yearly rhythm is the calendar of saints. Because there are so few heroes in today's world, we need the treasure we have in our saints. By incorporating their feast days into church functions and liturgies, another part of our history finds its way into everyday life.

So, putting everything together as a liturgist involves keeping many things in mind and finding ways to prepare parish celebrations that fit your situation. By keeping in mind liturgical principles and the need for cohesive celebrations, and by using the seasons to your advantage, the path to good liturgy becomes clearer. This does not mean easier — just less confusing. And once assemblies become accustomed to good liturgies, most will be ready, willing and able to help continue to make it so.

Looking at the Process

As we come into this process we call liturgy planning, it is important to remember several things—especially that we don't know it all. This is especially true when we are beginning but remains true all our lives. It is also important to remember that although our pastors don't know everything either, they didn't become priests without an education that included the study of liturgy. They have spent their entire professional lives involved in liturgy.

Clergy-bashing seems very much in vogue lately. There is a sense in some quarters that the laity could do a better job, are more tuned in, are more up-to-date on liturgy, and other equally nonsensical notions. This us-versus-them attitude is destructive to the very fabric of liturgy and in fact to the whole Body of Christ. Clergy and laity need one another in liturgy as in life itself. If we are to serve God and the Body of Christ, we must recognize that need, nurture it and work as a team.

Nothing I have seen is more destructive to liturgical renewal than the attitude of "it's just the priests who are holding us back." Granted, there are some who are more liturgically sensitive than others, but I've often wondered if some priests are antagonistic about working with lay liturgists because they have had a bad experience with someone who thought they knew best and lacked respect for the knowledge and authority of priests. But that isn't an excuse for those priests who refuse to cooperate in any way with improving their parish's liturgy. Some simply are not willing to make any changes. That's when the serenity prayer helps: Lord, grant me the courage to change the things I can, the serenity to accept the things I cannot change, and the wisdom to know the difference.

In the end, a collaborative ministry between clergy and laity, each respecting the position and knowledge of the other and willing to learn from the other, results in a win-win situation for everyone involved. We all have our roles, and none of them is unimportant.

With that in mind, there is another aspect of working together that is also true: Not everyone is going to get along, and not every group will work well together. For whatever reason — personality clashes, uncooperative attitudes or an unwillingness to share the planning process — there may come a time or place at which you simply cannot minister as a liturgist. It can be very destructive to everyone involved to continue in conflict. For your own sanity and spiritual life, you may need to decide whether you can live with the situation or if it is time to "shake the dust from your feet and move on." The only failure in such a situation is the failure to learn from the experience.

The planning process requires a great degree of flexibility, a willingness to look at every situation with an open mind and a prayerful attitude. What works with one pastor may not work with another. What works in one time or place may not work in another. Even the most successful "script" for a seasonal liturgical celebration may need fine-tuning from year to year to accommodate changes in circumstances. Some outside event may require immediate liturgical attention. A festive confirmation service may need to be changed or postponed after a community disaster. As spiritual needs change, liturgy needs to adapt to meet those needs.

In the final analysis, it is necessary to remember that when all the planning and preparing are finished and the liturgy begins, it is out of your hands. This celebration is offered to God, not to you or to the presider. You are part of the worshiping Body of Christ at this point, and you can trust that the grace of God and the power of the Holy Spirit will take it from here.

The Mass is our Lord's word, our Lord's meal, our Lord's presence. It is also our presence to each other and to the Lord. We plan and prepare to the best of our ability with prayerful attention to God's agenda for any particular liturgy. But when the time comes, we need to stand back and let God's agenda, not our individual agenda, take over. The Spirit is an ephemeral thing; it cannot be contained and controlled. By cooperating with this creating force, liturgy may surprise you. Our best liturgies have been ones that didn't go exactly according to plan but in which the Holy Spirit was clearly in charge and the whole became much more than the sum of its parts.

●

1 General Norms for the Liturgical Year and Calendar, #*1*.

2 *Another resource for exploring the deeper meaning of the seasons is a four-volume set of books by Adrian Nocent,* The Liturgical Year *(Collegeville, MN: The Order of St. Benedict, 1977). These books cover Advent-Christmas, Lent, The Easter Season and Ordinary Time. They give a biblical-liturgical reflection of the season and specific feasts plus the structure and themes for each season and feast. There is a biblical analysis for each Sunday and feast day of the liturgical year. While they may go a little deeper than most of us require, there are some good insights in the reflections.*

CHAPTER 7

The Downsizing Dilemma

We Have a Treasure

Much of what has been discussed up to this point applies to some extent to parishes of all sizes, with specific comments directed to the differences in small parishes. But the very act of downsizing liturgies to fit each parish is a problem in itself. Every parish is unique and has its own needs, expectations and character. No one approach will fit all situations, and there is no one perfect solution.

It is easy to think that prior to Vatican II all parishes looked alike, but that was no more true then than it is now. Each parish had its own approach to liturgy, usually the pastor's determination or interpretation of the "right way" to do things. Although the actual rituals were more standardized, this had more to do with conciliar and episcopal decrees, the training and education of priests, and also the fact that the pastor was, then, the only one in the parish making liturgical decisions. There were no committees to give input. But make no mistake — those things that were important to Father Kelly were done his way, which may or may not have been exactly the way Father Brown would have done them.

With the advent of liturgical reform, many people threw the "liturgical norm" out the window, and we went through a period of experimentation and constant change. Some of this was very good, and some of it was very bad. Unfortunately, some of the very bad is still with us because "we've always done it like this!" Thus we have wide variations in our approach to ritual.

So how does this impact the small parish? We have fewer resources to work with, often less exposure to "modern" liturgy and have learned to make do with what we have. Talking about improving ritual celebrations may not seem to have much relevance in our individual situations, but each parish has to look at its rituals and celebrations in light of the universal picture given in the liturgical documents and evaluate how they measure up. Then we need to decide where and how we can make them better. If we are to be a truly universal church, our liturgies must reflect our traditions regardless of size or location.

Just as the approach that works in a 2000-family parish won't work in a 200-family parish, the 200-family parish will differ from the 100-family parish. Not all small parishes are created equal. The criteria mentioned in chapter one — location and character, as well as size — have a major impact on the liturgies celebrated.

The history of our liturgy, with all its rituals, rites and symbols, is a treasury of riches. Each celebration is a multi-faceted jewel. These jewels are not reserved for those parishes with the wealth to access them — rather, they are there for all of us to learn about and enjoy.

It is like a family that has an old tray, dull and blackened, that has been on the sideboard for years. Everyone knows it belonged to their great-great grandmother, and so it is very meaningful to them. But it has never been used. It is regarded as "too precious to touch." And besides, it's ugly! Then one day, a new daughter-in-law sees the tray. Recognizing it as similar to one in her family, she takes it into the kitchen and with some polish and hard work has it gleaming. As she brings the now sparkling silver tray into the dining room, the family is amazed at the intricate detail that had been covered with years of tarnish from lack of use. The beautiful tray becomes not just a special heirloom to be looked at from afar but a special tray to be used and enjoyed.

Our small parish liturgies all too often have become that old tarnished tray. We know of the treasure from our past, but the beautiful details have become obscured by the tarnish of disuse. So now we need to get out the polish and show people what a treasure they really have in their liturgy.

What Does Downsizing Look Like?

After the liturgical education and abilities of those responsible for any changes are determined (and enhanced where needed), the situation needs to be evaluated and priorities need to be set. What is the most important aspect of our celebration? We have reviewed the various ministries, noting that proclamation of the word and at least the minimum music requirements rank high in importance. If you can make only one change, what should it be?

Part of the dilemma is knowing that not everything can be done at once, or sometimes even at all. So what does a downsized liturgy look like? Most of the areas of ministry I have covered require at least some people to step forward and take part. Some of the resort parishes I have encountered don't have those people. One national park immediately comes to mind.

Grand Canyon had a circuit-riding priest and a few local rangers and employees who assemble on a regular basis. This was probably the most downsized liturgy I could imagine. But it was also a memorable liturgy. These people made use of whoever showed up for Mass. "Is there someone here who is a lector? We need you to help us out this morning. We also need a couple of eucharistic ministers. I'll be here in the hall; come and see me." After the presider put a few of the early arrivals to work setting up the altar area and the necessary chairs, he went to the hall area and, sure enough, three or four people approached him to fill the needed ministries for that morning. There was no choir, and the lector didn't chant or sing the psalm; but the priest led the Alleluia and eucharistic acclamations, and the assembled participants sang them, no accompaniment needed. For that hour, we *were* the Body of Christ gathered in that place.

This obviously isn't a parish that has to concern itself with any of the sacraments other than eucharist, but it does what it can — and to the best of its ability. Is it the ideal? Does it fulfill the "norm"? Under these circumstances, yes. Is it the appropriate response in a parish with full-time members and a regular meeting place? Probably not.

What about the Midwestern diocese in which one priest and his assistant, who plays the organ, tend to three different parishes? Each parish has its own lay leader who looks after the day-to-day life of the parish, its own lectors and its own eucharistic ministers. One even has a choir. The organist is their choir director and cantor. In the parishes with no choirs, the organist plays and leads the people. The other ministries — altar servers, sacristan, ushers, art and environment — are performed in an informal manner, as needed. Each of these parishes has a different character. One has a well-organized ministry program, another has minimal lay ministry — doing only what it has to do, but no more — with one lector who does Mass every week and no eucharistic ministers at all.

One of the poorest examples of downsizing I've seen is also in a resort parish. The parish is large enough to support a lovely church, but I'm not sure that what they have there really constitutes a parish community. A circuit-riding priest comes every Sunday for a specific Mass. When I was there, the church was packed with people, some even standing outside the doors. Due to traffic, the priest was about ten minutes late. When he arrived, he had to set up the altar, vest and take every part of the Mass himself; there were no lectors, servers, ministers or even ushers. Under the circumstances, he did a good job. The homily showed preparation and thought; if he and given the same homily in three other parishes, or if he was bored, it didn't show. One wonders where all the local Catholics were and why there was no attempt to make their liturgical life their own. I hope to go back some-day to see if things have changed. I hope so, for these folks have a wonderful opportunity to show some genuine hospitality in a very busy resort.

Fewer Bodies, Scarce Resources

Perhaps the biggest challenge in a small parish is to find enough people to do what needs to be done. All of the liturgical resources will tell you that a person should only be involved in one ministry — if you are a lector, you can't also be a eucharistic minister or choir mem-ber. Granted, you can't do them all in the same liturgy, but most small parishes don't have the luxury of such limited involvement. Most of our lectors are also ushers and eucharistic ministers. It makes sched-uling a bit trickier, but there is rarely an overlap, except for the ushers. Sometimes a lector also takes up the collection. The only time we have a real problem is when the assigned minister is not present. (In unpredictable winter weather, it does happen.) All the lectors are trained to be prepared to proclaim the word at any Mass they attend; so, at least at the main Masses on Sundays, there are lectors.

Another common occurrence in smaller parishes is multiple ministers in the same family. We try to schedule all family members for the same Mass to avoid extra trips to church and also so that they may minister together or worship together as a family. When a family has small children, we schedule ministerial duties to ensure that one parent is with the children. What an example for them! They learn from an early age that Mass isn't just something we have to do on Sunday; it is a part of our lives, and we all have the responsibility to minister to one another.

Involving our young people in liturgy helps them incorporate faith and worship into their own lives, not just their parents' lives. These young people also fill a very real need. In a small parish, they are a necessary asset for providing ministers. Though young children cannot be eucharistic ministers, they are able to greet people and assist with the collection. Once children reach the age at which they can read — and understand what they read — they can be wonderful lectors. It is refreshing to the adult members of the assembly to hear the word proclaimed by a fresh, innocent face: Rather like Jesus teaching in the temple, isn't it?

There is no hard and fast rule about the age for lectors; it depends on ability. Schools are excellent resources for potential lectors. The teachers, both in public schools and in religious education classes, know which of their students excel in reading. Young people, however, may need sufficient training in using the microphone properly and speaking clearly. If some of your high-school-age students are involved in drama or speech classes, they already have the basic training for speaking in public and need only liturgical training for their role as lector.

There may be high-school-age people who can be eucharistic ministers. This is their church too, and we need their participation to be complete. But you will have to seek them out — very few young people will come to you to volunteer. They are as much afraid of rejection as you and I, probably more.

Having multiple ministers within families presents yet another problem for small parishes. If a family moves away, you may find yourself short in several ministries at the same time. We had one family in which the parents were both eucharistic ministers. Dad also did much of the ladder work for art and environment and assisted with altar servers. Mom was also in charge of religious education. One son was the senior server and acted much like a sacristan in setting up for all the Masses, and another was a musician. Their daughter was active in the youth group. This family was involved in almost every activity in the parish in some way. When they left, it was really a blow to our community. The loss left gaping holes in every area of ministry as well as in our faith community.

Consequently, we need to be flexible in our approach to staffing. What works this year may not work next year. Although people move around in large parishes too, the basic program usually doesn't change. If one coordinator leaves, that person is replaced. In a small parish, if a coordinator leaves, there may not be someone else who can step in right away.

The area of resources can pose a major dilemma for a small parish attempting to improve its liturgical program. Nothing comes cheap. I am constantly in awe of the amount of time, talent and money volunteered in our parish. We don't really have a liturgy budget as such; rather, we know what items we need each year and get them. If our needs are beyond the usual ones, we have to get creative.

We don't have funds for banners or special vesture. But we do have several good people who enjoy doing the sewing needed, and they frequently donate both time and material for projects. We have had people make the altar linens and even embroider the little crosses on the corporals. New choir folders were provided by a choir member who could get them at a discount. We also do many things related to hospitality, such as provide fresh rolls or muffins after church or soup suppers during Lent. Individuals bake goodies for Sunday mornings, and meals seem to materialize when needed. And so it goes; needs are taken care of, in spite of a shortage of funds.

There should be a brief word here about hospitality. Because it doesn't seem specifically connected to liturgy, it is frequently overlooked as part of liturgical ministry. But in a small parish, especially one where there are many visitors, the little touches — friendly greetings, assistance with the location of facilities, a personal invitation to join the "regulars" for coffee after Mass — are especially important. Even if there are no visitors, this weekly hospitality and socializing helps keep the community bonded as a family. So the seemingly small task of baking muffins is a needed part of building and nurturing community.

Not all things needed can be donated, however. Again, it becomes a matter of priorities. After the necessary costs to keep the physical plant operating — gas, electric, phone, maintenance, salaries, and so on — liturgy is the biggest cost for most parishes. Maybe the pew resources, such as the music books or missalettes, are outdated or not even used. Take inventory of what you have, and decide what you need. Then shop around. At the end of this book is a list of several companies that provide music and missalette resources. One will have a program that is right for your parish, and most will work with you to get the most for your money.

If you have older hardcover hymnals that are no longer used, advertise in your diocesan paper to see if someone else could use them. They may be just what another parish is looking for but can't afford to buy new. They will get a resource, and you will get some cash for something that was just collecting dust. The same approach in reverse may help you find needed resources at a reduced price.

Scarce resources also refers to staff people with the necessary education and training. In years past we just assumed that people would donate their time and talent to the church, and in that belief we have taken advantage of many fine people. If someone has spent time and money to receive an education and depends on that to make a living, justice demands that we look at equitable salaries. The positions that come to mind include organists and specially trained musicians, youth ministers and directors of religious education. It could even include liturgists! Very few small parishes can afford to pay someone for these positions, but at some point in your liturgical and educational growth, they will be needed.

One solution we came up with was to join with two other small parishes in the area and hire one director of religious education. She supervised the classes for sacramental preparation and the religious education programs for all three parishes, and she trained others to teach and lead. She was an excellent catechist with the necessary education to head such a program, but she certainly could not afford to do it for free. This way, all three parishes got much better programs than they could have achieved on their own, and one of our own didn't have to leave the area to get a job.

These same three parishes then hired a trained youth minister. Most of the kids went to the same high school, but no one parish had enough high school students to have much of a program. So it was natural to combine them into one group. So far, it has been successful.

Don't let lack of funds keep you from improving your liturgy. Most changes and growth require more time and hard work than money, and by now you have discovered that being a liturgist requires a lot of both time and work!

Smaller, Not Less

It is very easy to get hung up on numbers. But it is quality that counts, not quantity. With a few people who are truly committed and interested more can be achieved than with a large number of people who are only mildly interested and unwilling to commit.

In your lector program, for example, three or four committed and well-trained people proclaiming God's word will do more to enhance your liturgies than having many readers, some of whom stumble through or read in a monotone without a clue as to what it means to proclaim the word. Those three or four will probably inspire others to join them, but until that happens, rejoice in what you have. It's less stressful and more productive than worrying about what you don't have.

As a parish, it has taken us a while to learn to judge the success of special liturgies not by how many people come but rather by how God was able to touch the lives of those who were there. We have had a truly moving and effective anointing service with fewer than 20 people present, including the ministers. A Tuesday evening Bible study may not have a large turnout, but it does have a great deal of impact on the lives of those participating. They in turn have an impact on the rest of the community.

Part of the dilemma of downsizing liturgy is setting priorities. This doesn't mean eliminating rituals but rather keeping them appropriate for the size of the parish. It means having only the number of Masses actually needed, especially for days like Christmas, Easter and holy days. It means making your schedule for everything from Masses to meetings fit the lives of your people. Most parishes have meetings going on every evening of the week. We try to have as many things as possible after Sunday Mass or on one or two evenings a month.

We hold choir practice the hour before Mass on Sunday. Our people don't want to have to come out during the week because of the distance and weather. However, we do call special rehearsals for Advent/Christmas and Lent/Easter. We all agree on a day and time, and because it happens only occasionally, we get good cooperation.

There normally isn't enough business to attend to or decisions to be made to require council meetings every week — or even every month. If you were to look at diocesan guidelines for the structure of a parish, it would be difficult to imagine how our parish functions. But if you look at the results, we do quite well. An advantage to being small is that everyone sees everyone else on Sunday. So minor items can be handled on the spot, or a decision can be made to call a meeting and a consensus on a day and time can be reached.

In the area of liturgy, we are able to have infant baptisms during Mass because there is rarely more than one and usually not more than one a month. In my former, large parish, we had 12 to 15 every other week! We can utilize all our liturgical resources for one festive Christmas Eve service and gather as one family. Do we do all the rituals? We do all that are required and as many options as we are able. We even had the Proclamation of Christmas chanted last year. Our services may not be overflowing with people, but everyone has a seat, and the visitors among us stand out and are welcomed.

Small parishes need to look closely at what is required for good liturgy and then do it well. When we have the people with the ability to do so, we take full advantage of the options offered. For example, our former pastor could not sing, not even a little, and we had no deacon. We did have a good cantor, though, so we took advantage of the option to have a lay person chant the Exultet at the Easter Vigil rather than having the pastor simply read it. It made for a much fuller experience of this special night.

Many resources on proclaiming the word suggest that there should be two separate people proclaiming the first reading and the second reading. Sometimes for a special feast we can do that, but for every week, we are happy to have a different lector at each Mass. Is our liturgy poorer for not having two lectors? I don't think so.

When you hear about or experience something special in a large parish, don't assume you can't do it in your parish. See what made that experience special or meaningful, then make what changes are needed to accommodate your size without losing that which made it special in the first place. We attended a penance service that was built around the paschal candle and readings that emphasized walking out of darkness into light. The readings were proclaimed from many places in the church. As a specially prepared examination of conscience was read, people brought up votive candles to place around the paschal candle. It was very effective, and we wanted to bring it home to our parish. But, instead of having 300 people present, we could count on maybe 20.

We were renovating our worship space at the time and had no fixed pews. Taking advantage of that, we placed chairs in a circle around the paschal candle and surrounded it with large clay containers filled with votive candles. The readings were proclaimed by people from their places in various parts of the circle. Following a time of silence, we used a simple psalm refrain between each reading. The examination of conscience was broken up into individual statements and questions, each assigned to a different person, including children. Each person was asked to light a votive candle; each candle added to the light in the room. It was the transformation of darkness to light, in conjunction with the readings, that had been effective in the first service, and it was equally so in our small group.

The dilemma of downsizing isn't that good liturgy can't be done but rather that it requires a more creative approach. And that ability to adapt and be creative requires a sound understanding of the basic principles, rubrics and symbols of liturgy. My pastor always asks for the meaning behind what is being proposed, what we are trying to convey. Sometimes it is clear to us but would be lost or confusing to others. The question must always be: How does this bring the dying and rising of Christ to the people in a way that touches their everyday lives?

There is another important point that needs emphasizing: Don't make something or use something that is cheap simply to *have something*. Everything used for liturgy must reflect the sacredness of its purpose. One well-made item is better than a sanctuary full of cheap bric-a-brac. "Liturgy . . . demands quality and appropriateness. The first rules out anything trivial and self-centered, anything fake, cheap or shoddy, anything pretentious or superficial. . . . The second point refers to the physical environment of public worship and to any art forms which might be employed as part of the liturgical action (e.g., ritual movement, gestures, audio-visuals, etc.)."[1]

This means quality lectionaries, not throwaway paper missalettes. How is the importance of the word of God symbolized when that word is not important enough to warrant a quality vessel? It means real flowers, not plastic ones, even though the quantity may be much less. It means replacing worn-out vestments and sacred books. Our symbols, including our gestures and our environment, must speak to us of all that is holy, not all that is economical.

So with downsizing there is bad news and there is good news. The bad news is that with limited resources, you can't have everything you want when you want it. The good news is that you have the flexibility to be very creative and very pastoral. By being involved in a small parish, we know the problems, the hurts, the joys and the journeys of our communities well enough to be able to recognize the incarnation of Christ's dying and rising, God's love for all of us, in *this* time, in *this* place, in *this* liturgy.

●

1 Environment and Art in Catholic Worship, *nos. 20, 22, 23.*

CHAPTER 8

Celebrating the Seasons

High Holy Days

Although the church year actually begins with Advent, our observance of the Easter Triduum (meaning "Three Days") is the summit of our celebration. These three days are often referred to as the hinge-pin of the liturgical year and the fulcrum of our spiritual lives. Think about it: The death and resurrection of Jesus Christ is the reason we have a religion called Christianity. We celebrate this dying and rising every Sunday, but the Triduum is the high point of the year and a logical starting point from which to examine specific liturgies.

When we talk about High Holy Days, we tend to think of the Jewish celebrations of Rosh Hashanah and Yom Kippur. These are the celebrations of the New Year and the Day of Atonement. "These are profoundly serious days, with a feeling of the heavy moral responsibility which life puts on all. . . . They are concerned only with the life of the individual, with his religious feelings and innermost probings. It [the period of Rosh Hashanah and Yom Kippur] is greeted not with noise and joy, but with a serious and contrite heart."[1]

In our Catholic faith, the term "high holy days" refers to the three-day period of the Triduum. Just as Rosh Hashanah and Yom Kippur are the hinge-pin of Jewish spiritual life, the Triduum is the hinge-pin of ours. It celebrates everything that makes us Christian, our very reason for being.[2]

It is easy to think of Lent and Easter as two separate seasons, but in reality they make up one long season that begins on Ash Wednesday and concludes with Pentecost. Because there are so many different liturgies involved, in large parishes they are frequently divided up among various members of a liturgy committee. This sometimes results in less unification of the season as a whole. An advantage in the small parish is that, because we don't have that many bodies, the same people will be involved in the planning process from beginning to end.

Why is it important to keep this sense of continuity? Because in order to be able to truly enter into the type of celebration we need for the Triduum, it is necessary to have a period of spiritual preparation. The magnitude of the Easter celebration cannot be contained in the short space of the Triduum and Easter Sunday. If we are to assist our assemblies in coming to a fuller understanding of this most important liturgical point of our year, our symbols and rituals must point us in that direction.

In current practice, the process of initiating new members culminates with their baptism and reception into the church at the Easter Vigil. The period of Lent is the final period of preparation. "Lent is a preparation for the celebration of Easter, for the Lenten liturgy disposes both catechumens and the faithful to celebrate the paschal mystery: catechumens, through the several stages of Christian initiation; the faithful, through reminders of their own baptism and through penitential practices."[3] This is a time for us, as liturgists, to let our people know that this is a season to be taken seriously. It is a time to stop hiding behind the facade of everyday life (or the usual environment in our church) and come face to face with our sinfulness and our hope.

How can we help? When people enter the worship space on Ash Wednesday, if everything not essential is gone and the place looks empty, it is a strong visual cue that this liturgy is not just business as usual. We can use unaccompanied singing or chant to emphasize further the stripping away of the usual. Above all, Ash Wednesday should not be a day when people come just to "get their ashes." A community liturgy reminds us that Lent is not just a time for personal confession and repentance but also a time to recognize our communal shortcomings too.

In recent years there has been a resurgence of the "Order of Penitents," Catholics who have been separated from the church for whatever reason and now wish to join in full communion again. Their time for final preparation is during Lent and culminates with their being received back to the Lord's table on Holy Thursday. There is a model here for parishes, too. In recent years we have focused the period of Lent as one long penitential service. We use the liturgy on Ash Wednesday to emphasize the beginning of a journey of self-examination, confession, repentance and reconciliation, and individual confessions are encouraged during this forty-day period. Our penitential rites and prayers of the faithful reflect a communal as well as a personal soul-searching during the Sundays of Lent.

One way we have fostered continuity and ritual recognition of the season is through music. For the past four or five years, we have used the same set of eucharistic acclamations. We start singing this set of acclamations on Ash Wednesday and continue with them through Pentecost. During Lent, we use the first eucharistic prayer of reconciliation with music written for that prayer called the "Mass of Remembrance," by Marty Haugen.[4] The music is written so that, if you have a pastor who sings well, the entire eucharistic prayer can be sung or chanted with several interspersed acclamations sung by the assembly. It is also very effective when spoken with the sung acclamations, which are easy to learn. During the Easter season, we use the same acclamations interspersed within Eucharistic Prayer I.

This change of music at the start of Lent is another cue that something new has begun. Because we use it year after year, it has become part of our prayer life. We don't have to think about the music; we just pray it.

Another musical cue we employ is using simple music, perhaps a refrain only, as a gathering song. "Song of the Body of Christ" works very well.[5] We add a simple communion song and either silence or a closing song that speaks of our hope. We frequently use the same music for the entire Lenten season but with a different choir piece that reflects the readings each week. The whole focus of our liturgical choices reflects a simplification that engenders prayer.

As we come to the end of Lent, we begin to focus on our Lord's passion. Passion (Palm) Sunday is the final transformation, beginning with the joyous celebration of Christ's entry into Jerusalem and ending with his death. It is a very powerful liturgy, but it is important not to put all the emphasis on the palm procession and forget the power in the rest of the liturgy. In a small parish setting, you may be able to do a very symbolic procession in which you actually make your way through town. It is a strong witness to others to see a whole parish, accompanied by song, making its way through the streets with banners and incense and palms waving.

Once the procession has ended and the liturgy of the word begins, the mood changes abruptly. Take advantage of this with your best lectors and cantor. The psalm for the day, Psalm 22, is one of the most powerful of all. Choosing a very somber setting, such as Christopher Walker's "My God, My God," stresses the contrast between the joyous entry and the passion.[6] The passion can be proclaimed by the presider or deacon, or it can be done in parts by two lectors and the celebrant with the assembly included. It is generally set out in this fashion in booklets for the people. But however it is done, the proclamation should make full use of the mysteries of human life tied into the celebration of the passion. This liturgy really plunges us into the passion and prepares us for the beginning of the Triduum on Holy Thursday.

"The Easter Triduum of the passion and resurrection of Christ is the culmination of the entire liturgical year."[7] Thus the document *General Norms for the Liturgical Year* gives the Triduum the same prominence in the church year that Sunday has in the week. It may take several years to help a community understand that this is one celebration over three nights. But once they do, those who attend will be there out of desire, and on Easter Sunday there will be a bond among them that has nothing to do with lack of sleep!

In a small parish it is not difficult to follow the rubrics of the sacramentary and have as full a celebration as any large parish. It can be more intimate, though. In our parish we no longer wash the feet of twelve men on Holy Thursday. In the fullness of the symbol, the presider, as Christ's example, renders this service to others — all who are seated at the ends of the pews on the center aisle have their feet washed: men, women and children. This, more than any words, makes a lasting impression on our young people. We don't tell them they are included; we simply include them. To focus attention on this ritual, we don't sing. The organist plays a quiet piece of music so that the people, including the choir, don't need to have their attention on a book but can be attentive to the ritual. A simple refrain could also be repeated throughout.

While washing the feet of every person is generally not practical, washing hands has no symbolism at all in this instance. The washing of feet is a humble service that requires the washer to kneel at the feet of the person being washed. Some parishes set up several stations for footwashing so that others in the community may also share in the ritual. Since time is not of the essence in this type of liturgy, take the time to do this ritual well. One note: Do not remove your pastor from the central role in this ritual. As the primary minister in your community, his example needs to be visible, and most pastors with whom I have spoken find in this ritual a genuine pastoral moment.

In a small parish, you may have to be very creative to find a location for the altar of repose. Please don't set aside part of the sanctuary. The current rubrics call for the tabernacle to be in another room altogether, although many small parishes have not yet been able to accomplish this ideal. And on this night in particular, the altar of repose *cannot* be the tabernacle and should be in another location. Try to arrange the procession so that all may take part. This may mean going out of the church, around it and back in again. Unless the weather is inclement, this is worth doing. This procession says again that we are not about business as usual.

The art and environment for Thursday should be kept simple; it must be stripped away after the service and the church left completely bare for Good Friday. The Good Friday service should be very simple. This is a good time to use unaccompanied singing. Veneration of the cross is easily accomplished in a smaller setting with the use of only one cross, without a corpus: This is a time to venerate the instrument by which our salvation came. Again, the proclamation of the passion is the high point of the liturgy. In years past we have involved all of our cantors and proclaimed the gospel as a choral reading, assigning different parts to different voices. Traditionally, the people follow along in a book and have some lines themselves. But the gospel is meant to be heard, not read, especially at this liturgy. When your lectors are well-rehearsed, as they must be for this occasion, there is no need to read along. They will keep the assembly's attention!

The Easter Vigil on Saturday is the culmination of the Triduum and also of the entire church year. The *General Norms for the Liturgical Year and the Calendar* (GNLY) refers to it as the "mother of all vigils." The only difference between large and small parishes should be the number of those being initiated into the church on this night. Size is not an excuse to skimp on the fire, the readings or the rites. A large fire that everyone can gather around is the proper symbol with which to begin this celebration. A small fire in a hibachi or barbecue grill just doesn't have the same impact as a fire blazing into the sky.

The proclamation of the *Exultet* on this night is too important for it not to be sung. If you do not have a pastor or deacon who can sing, a lay person is permitted to do so by observing the rubric in the chant that applies when it is done by someone other than a priest or deacon. The chant setting in the sacramentary is not difficult and is quite compelling.

We have done all seven Old Testament readings for several years. The fact that our initiation rite involves fewer people allows more time for the readings. When it is explained, before Saturday night, that this is the one time each year when we hear our story from the beginning—and when it is *done well*—it is an experience, not an ordeal. We do each reading with different lectors. For some readings we use one, for others two, and for some, even three readers. *This is the Word of the Lord* is an excellent resource for readings in dialogue form.[8] Ours has been a tradition of oral storytelling since early Hebrew times.

A passage about beginning this night in the dark, from Gabe Huck's introduction to *Parish Path through Lent and Eastertime* (see note 2), resonated with me. We proclaim the first seven readings by the light of the paschal candle. The lectors are at the back of the church with a light on their stand so that the movement between readings isn't a distraction.

We use the same psalm response between each reading, eliminating the need for light to see the response. And we have used the same response for several years, so it is also part of the people's prayer. It was a difficult decision not to do each of the psalms in their entirety, and we may do them again. But in order to not overburden the people with words when we began doing all the readings, we chose the word over song. We keep the prayer between the readings and have a period of silence. It helps the continuity of the readings to not break them up excessively. The response has been overwhelmingly positive. It takes about an hour to complete the introductory rites and the liturgy of the word, but it doesn't seem that long.

We have also used slides with some of the readings. If you have the people and equipment to do it easily, this also can be an inspiring part of presenting our story, revealing the unique experience of the paschal mystery in this particular community. Because the church is darkened, slides make a good visual accompaniment to the readings. This may seem gimmicky, and it may not be appropriate for your community. But the whole point of these seven readings is to get the attention of the hearers, to draw them into the story and bring it to life. This is our history as a people, and it is heard only once a year.

As we move toward the light of the Risen Christ in our liturgy of the word, we sing the Gloria while the lights in the church come on. At the same time, the candles in the sanctuary are lighted and the bells of the church are rung. This makes full use of this symbolic movement from darkness into light.

We will discuss the initiation process in more detail in the next chapter, but it is an integral part of the Vigil. It is especially necessary to understand the entire ritual in order to make the necessary adaptations for small numbers of candidates. We have even had years in which no one came into the church, child or adult. But as part of the Vigil, the blessing of the water and the renewal of baptismal promises is vital. Work with the rituals and rubrics to adapt this part of the liturgy to your own needs. Remember that we are all part of the larger church and are thus praying for all those who join us on this night, wherever they may be.

The Triduum has many other possible additional liturgies or parish functions. However, it is best to do fewer and to do them well. We have a basic script that we use every year for these three days. There is no point to inventing the wheel anew every year. We are very careful about adding or changing any part of the liturgies, because the people now know what to expect, and things are familiar to them.

However, good ideas can be improved upon, and some changes will usually be necessary to keep the ritual current with needs and abilities. But if you do make changes, be sure they are well-reasoned and not just for the sake of change. Since we are different people in different circumstances each year, no two years will ever be exactly the same.

It also makes your and your pastor's life much less hectic to be able to pull out the script and see what has been done in the past rather than start over each year. After each season, get together with everyone involved and critique the liturgies. What worked well, and what did not work at all? What difficulties were encountered in carrying out the rite? Are there changes that need to be considered next year? It would be nice to think that we will remember how everything went this year when we begin preparing next year, but that's not realistic.

The same is true of additional functions or liturgies. Among the additional functions and liturgies we have added are a light supper on Thursday evening to begin our time together, soup suppers on Friday and Saturday evening in keeping with the paschal fast, stations of the cross on Friday and Liturgy of the Hours at various times. Morning prayer replaces our Friday and Saturday morning services, and night prayer ends the Thursday period of adoration as well as Friday's time of reflection at the cross. These special adaptations have helped emphasize our sense of community and continuity during the Triduum.

It is good to assign some of the additional liturgies to lay leaders. The Liturgy of the Hours and stations of the cross can be led very well by lay people. This not only gives them experience in a leadership role but relieves the pastor of additional burdens in an already busy time. A valuable resource for these and all special seasons is *Sourcebook for Sundays and Seasons*.[9]

Again, due to fewer numbers, many of these additional liturgies and functions may be less well attended. But they allow those present to celebrate on a deeper level. Numbers alone don't indicate success or failure. Some things need time to catch on. Our parish community felt the spiritual benefits all year after we began the suppers and Liturgy of the Hours. For many of our people, it was their first exposure to Liturgy of the Hours.

After all of this celebrating, we still have Easter Sunday and the Easter season. It is difficult to keep up the momentum for fifty days, but in terms of music and environment, this is a festive season. Musically, Easter Sunday is almost a repeat of the Vigil. Because our musicians are usually tired at this point after three nights of singing, keeping it simple is appreciated. There is a sequence between the second reading and the gospel acclamation; this should be sung. A setting of "Ye Sons and Daughters" works well here. By its nature, Easter Sunday is less complex than the Vigil, but bear in mind that for some people, this will be their only Easter celebration. Everything about this liturgy must be welcoming. If it is a positive experience and people feel welcome, they just might come back again before next Christmas or Easter!

Included in the Easter season is Ascension of the Lord. In some states it has been moved to the Seventh Sunday of Easter. But regardless of the date, it is another liturgy of celebration. It also follows the Easter theme of joy in the Risen Lord. One helpful characteristic of the Easter Season is that the environment stays the same. It doesn't change until Pentecost. Be sure someone is responsible for caring for the lilies and other fresh flowers. Drooping lilies and wilted arrangements encourage drooping and wilted liturgies. This is a season to use your most joyful music and most upbeat settings of the psalms. Keep the word "rejoice" in mind in all your planning.

The Easter season draws to a close with Pentecost. The environment changes, the colors going from white to red. But this isn't the sorrowful red of Good Friday: It is a joyful use of color — adding the red to the white and gold Easter decor emphasizes the continuity of the season. There is an expanded liturgy for the Vigil of Pentecost as well as a more elaborate liturgy for Sunday. This day, the liturgy of the word includes a sequence, just as is found on Easter Sunday. It should be sung, if at all possible. This celebration is very festive, but it is not a "birthday party" for the church. It is a celebration of Easter and of the gift of the Holy Spirit, which is ours by reason of our initiation. The celebration of the sacrament of confirmation for young people is also generally around this time. This liturgy of Pentecost can be used to bring together all those who were baptized or received into the church at the Easter Vigil, those who have just been confirmed or have celebrated their first communion, and all those babies who have been baptized in the past year. It is a celebration of hope and joy, and these people are living symbols at this liturgy. They are visible signs of the working of the Holy Spirit in our lives.

This season from Ash Wednesday through Pentecost is a quarter of our liturgical year. Is it any wonder that it requires so much effort? It demands our very best, but it pays off during the rest of the year. The spiritual benefits of a well-celebrated Lent and Eastertime will carry us forward into the challenges ahead.

Advent and Christmas

"Advent has a twofold character: as a season to prepare for Christmas when Christ's first coming to us is remembered; as a season when that remembrance directs the mind and heart to await Christ's Second Coming at the end of time. Advent is thus a period for devout and joyful expectation."[10] Again, it is necessary to cue the assembly that the liturgical time has changed. We are so inundated with Christmas, which begins before Halloween in many areas, that our liturgies have to work hard to keep the focus on Advent.

Art and environment are a big help in this season. Keeping things simple and removing what is not necessary is a helpful symbol for everyone. We do a physical housecleaning to prepare for the birth of our Lord just as we do a spiritual housecleaning. This is a time to get back to basics. It is the liturgical New Year, a time to take stock of where we are in our spiritual journey, a time to make new year's resolutions in our spiritual lives and review how we did on last year's.

This is perhaps the best time of year to emphasize that the liturgical cycle is not a circle but a spiral. Each revolution on a spiral brings you to the same point but on another level. Has there been growth since last year? This is one season for which bulletin inserts emphasizing the spiritual inventory and preparation of the season can be helpful tools.

Since we are competing with the secular culture during this season, it is important that nothing in our liturgies bring Christmas too soon. That means no evergreens or Christmas trees, no red or green decorations and no Christmas carols. Better no trees than to have them too soon. It robs us of an important time, the time to prepare. Yes, this is a very busy season for everyone, and it is countercultural not to celebrate Christmas all month long in December. But Christianity *is* countercultural.

Music is an important cue for people when it comes to recognizing seasons. We usually use one specific set of eucharistic acclamations for Advent and Christmas each year. Again, it provides seasonal recognition — something has changed — and it provides continuity between Advent and Christmas. Sometimes these cues work more on a subconscious level than on any other. But again, ritual is repetition. There is a familiarity, a sense of stability in this ritual repetition that is comforting in today's unstable world.

We can use music, environment and scripture coordinated with good homiletics to emphasize the preparation for the second coming of our Lord in the first weeks of Advent. The same can be used in the last weeks of Advent to prepare for the birth of our Lord, both historically and presently in our hearts and lives. Then on Christmas Eve, all is hushed and the church is transformed with white and gold, evergreens and candles. The babe is in the manger, and we proclaim his holy birth. Our environment should not try to rival Macy's but rather should reflect the dignity and simplicity of the nativity scene. White with gold and red accents are the proper colors of the season — not red and green! The transformation from the last Sunday of Advent to Christmas Eve should be as dramatic as the stripped church on the first Sunday of Advent.

In our parish, we not only gather early for a pre-liturgy service of carols and choir music, we also have hot coffee and cider going at the back of the church to be ready after Mass. It is a time of gathering as family. There are carols playing, encouraging us to take a few minutes before rushing home. We begin our celebration at 8:00 or 8:30 in the evening. This works better for us than having a traditional midnight Mass, which excludes many children and older parishioners. We also have only one Vigil Mass on Christmas Eve.

As a liturgical season, Christmas is relatively short. It runs from the Vigil of Christmas until the Baptism of the Lord. But because the secular world begins in October and stops abruptly on December 26, it is difficult to maintain the celebration. One way to preserve Advent and maintain Christmas is to schedule parish Christmas parties between Christmas and Epiphany. This not only relieves people (especially parents) of extra busy-ness and gives them time for spiritual preparation, it also accentuates our Christian perspective on Christmas.

During the Christmas season, we celebrate the sacred memorial of Christ's birth and early life. The GNLY tells us that next to the celebration of the paschal mystery, we hold most sacred this natal celebration. There aren't enough Sundays in this season to use all the familiar music. If the pace of life in your parish will allow it, this is a wonderful time to gather for community suppers and carol-singing. In many areas, we have to contend with winter weather that may hamper extra efforts; but if we are to help our children realize that Christmas isn't just Santa and lots of goodies, we need to be sure that Jesus Christ gets as much exposure as Santa Claus.

Ordinary Time

There are 33 or 34 weeks that are not part of specific seasons and do not celebrate a specific aspect of the mystery of Christ. Instead, they are devoted to celebrating all aspects of the mystery of Christ. They are the Sundays in Ordinary Time, and the color for these Sundays is green.

We use the word "ordinary" in the secular vernacular to mean commonplace, average, usual, mundane or even dull. However, in liturgical terms it derives from the term ordinal, meaning numbered. Let us hope that celebrating the dying and rising of Jesus Christ is never commonplace or mundane, and especially not dull! Sundays in Ordinary Time are ordinal, or counted, and specifically referred to by number — the Twenty-fourth Sunday of the year, for example.

It is during this period of Ordinary Time that we also find the sanctoral calendar known as the Calendar of Saints. Some specific saint is recognized on most days. On Sundays and solemnities, memorials of saints are not celebrated unless specifically noted, such as on the Feast of Saints Peter and Paul (June 29). However, the feast days of the patrons of your diocese and parish should be noted and celebrated. Most of us are fairly unaware of this concurrent Calendar of Saints.

There is a definite order of celebrations in Ordinary Time. It is found in chapter two of GNLY, in the "Table of Liturgical Days According to their Order of Preference." This (and all pertinent liturgical documents) may be found in most sacramentaries. The feast for your parish's patron saint may be a special day of celebration for your parish, including a special liturgy. Each saint is listed in the Proper of Saints in the sacramentary with the appropriate prayers. We try to have a special liturgy and a parish picnic on the Sunday closest to our patron saint's day. This is another reason to become very familiar with the sacramentary, lectionary and ordo.

Also within the cycle of Ordinary Time, there are "little seasons" in the gospel readings. Each annual cycle uses a different gospel: Year A is the Gospel of Matthew, Year B is Mark and Year C is Luke. Each year also has intermittent passages from the Gospel of John. Beginning on the Third Sunday in Ordinary Time, a semi-continuous reading of the gospel for that year of the cycle takes place. The readings after Epiphany deal with the beginning of the Lord's preaching. At the end of the year, the gospels deal with eschatological or end-time themes.

While Ordinary Time presents its own choices and challenges, in the main it remains less festive in nature than Christmas and Eastertime and lacks the introspection expected during Advent and Lent.

In small parishes, and I suspect in large parishes also, it is easy to let down in Ordinary Time. But each liturgy needs attention to be the best possible celebration of the Lord's Day. Paying attention to the readings and choosing appropriate music can make this a special time in its own right.

Penitential and Anointing Services

In our human condition, we often stand in need of healing of both body and soul. In the sacraments of reconciliation and anointing, the church has provided a ritual setting for these needs. They are rich liturgies that need to be used often and well.

In today's world, the facts of sin and evil are all too obvious. We strive as Christians to overcome this human condition, but there are times when we need to say, "I'm sorry." We need to say this to God and to one another. We need to do it alone with our God and with one another gathered in community.

There are times when we need the guidance of a confessor. These are private times during which we don't need to concern ourselves with liturgical matters other than to be sure there is a time and a conducive place in our community for this sacrament. The environment of the reconciliation room must convey the love and mercy of the God who calls us there. Thus, care must be taken to be sure it is an inviting place, not a forbidding one. But our liturgical responsibilities end at the door.

In every Mass there is a penitential rite to reminds us that we have fallen short and are in need of God's forgiving grace. As liturgists we must take care that this rite is a considered part of planning, using the option most appropriate to the season and circumstance. There may be circumstances in which specially written petitions are needed for this rite. But again, our role here is limited.

More and more we are becoming aware that there is a definite communal aspect to sin. We don't sin in a vacuum, but rather our sins affect those around us, and we are affected by the sins of others. Vatican II specifically called for the rite and formularies for the sacrament of penance to be revised so that they express more clearly the nature and effect of the sacrament (see the *Constitution on the Sacred Liturgy,* #71). The support of our community is important in strengthening us to avoid sin, and it is important in helping us reconcile with God and with one another.

In a small parish, regular penance services provide a setting to build the trust in one another that promotes healing. Most of the problems of everyday life result from a thoughtless word, a failure to treat each other with kindness or a choice that doesn't reflect our commitment for good. A penance service is structured to help us recall those times and move toward reconciliation. More properly, they are reconciliation services — our aim is not to sit around and focus on our failures but to focus on the mercy of a forgiving and loving God.

If you count success by numbers, the small parish is doomed to failure in these services. We have rarely had more than 25 or 30 people in attendance, although it goes in cycles. Some of the most meaningful services have been very small and personal. In a large crowd it is easy to disconnect from the community and focus on your personal failings. In a small gathering, you are face to face with your friends and family.

Music plays a role in these services, as does the choice of scripture. The purpose is to help people look at areas where they need improvement and also to help them know that God is there with forgiveness and healing. Music can help set the mood of the service, and the season can influence your choice for readings. For example, the Advent season is an appropriate time to focus on returning to the love of the Lord or walking in the Light of Christ. Lent lends itself to the theme of a journey toward reconciliation. As a theme, "forsaking the darkness of sin to walk in the light of Christ" is always relevant. The examination of conscience is likewise written to guide people in the general direction of the season.

In a penitential service, as in all liturgies, there is a structure, an order, to worship. It begins with a gathering song to focus on our purpose for this liturgy, a greeting and an opening prayer by the presider followed by scripture readings. There is an examination of conscience and prayers of intercession, then a communal act of contrition followed by the invitation to individual confession. We then regather for a song of thanksgiving and closure of the liturgy. Within this structure is room for adaptation. Any of these elements can be tailored to suit a specific community at a specific time with a specific need. These are the basic structures, but the ways in which you use them are open to creativity. You have a great deal of flexibility in choosing readings, for example. On this, *The Rites* has a section on penance that is quite thorough.[11] It states that the readings should (a) let God's voice be heard calling people back to conversion, (b) call to mind the mystery of our reconciliation, and (c) bring to bear on people's lives God's judgment of good and evil as a light for the examination of conscience.

For some services I have used all gospel readings followed by a reflection. At other times I have chosen readings in groups, such as an Old Testament reading of prophecy followed by a New Testament reading of fulfillment. Sometimes these readings have had a specific musical piece repeated between them, such as a psalm refrain sung by all. One year we used "Salvatore Mundi" from the Taizé collection.

We also try always to have a specific action for the penitents, such as lighting votive candles or performing a ritual hand-washing. Be careful not to be "gimmicky"; the action must make sense in light of the entire service and, of course, the tradition of Christian celebration. We make provision for individual confessions with soft music playing. It is a quiet time for prayer and reflection for everyone, whether they are going to confession or not. We then conclude with prayer and song.

Creating an examination of conscience that involves questions by different people and prayers of petition to answer those questions can be effective in getting more people really involved and participating in the liturgy. Many books contain prepared reconciliation services. *The Rites,* mentioned above, has a very detailed outline for services, including suggested prayers and readings and examples of general confessions. It is well worth becoming familiar with this resource, not just for this rite but for all rites.

The book *Penitential Services* has served me well over the years.[12] I have adapted the services by using parts of several. Having a good resource is not only helpful but also time-saving. Trying to compose each prayer or question is frustrating. Very good ones have already been composed and can be used or adapted to fit your unique needs for reconciliation services and your particular situation.

When it is time for children's first celebration of reconciliation, we structure the service so that it is meaningful for them and they feel support from the whole community. It is important to help them remember, and to remind ourselves, that just as our sin affects others, our return to the light brightens the way for others. A room dimly lit during confessions that becomes brighter with each votive candle lighted by the reconciled is a strong visual symbol that needs no explanation, even for children.

The sacrament of anointing has a long history and has taken many forms. During the decades before Vatican ii, it was generally done as part of the ritual called viaticum, which took place near the time of death. It was a beautiful private ritual performed either in the hospital or in the home with a few family members, if they were available. Thus for many people, this sacrament still bears the stigma of pending death. Vatican ii simplified the rite of anointing and clearly distinguished it from viaticum, which is administered when death is imminent and is a separate rite with different prayers. The emphasis in viaticum is on the passage from life to death. Anointing is for those whose "health is seriously impaired by sickness or old age."[13]

Thus, anointing is no longer something done privately and only near the point of death. It is becoming recognized as a source of strength and healing for all in times of serious illness. As such, it is properly done with the support of the community. It can be a formal service announced and planned with the full ritual and music, or it can be done as part of a Mass or after Mass as needed. Even when it is done for a member of the community who is in a hospital or at home, it is especially meaningful if there are at least some members of the community present. Don't ever doubt the power of prayer and this sacrament. Its ability to comfort the afflicted goes beyond words.

There are resources available to assist in preparing a specific liturgy for the Rite of Anointing. The first place to look is, again, the book *The Rites.* It includes outlines and examples of anointing outside Mass, within Mass and in a hospital setting. While the sacrament of penance is not formally included in the rite, the directives make it clear that the opportunity for penance must also be available, preferably prior to the Rite of Anointing and otherwise during the penitential rite. Explore the richness of this liturgy. It can be especially effective in the small parish setting because we are close to one another, and giving comfort to one another is part of that closeness. This ancient ritual reacquaints us with our role of praying for and healing each other.

There is a simple but beautiful setting of the Rite of Anointing with music by Andrew J. Witchger.[14] It also has text for non-singing priests, but the people's responses can still be sung. We first experienced this setting at the National Association of Pastoral Musicians convention in Saint Louis in 1993. Several thousand people attended that liturgy, but good planning and this musical setting made it very moving. I have since used it in our parish, where it has been very effective with as few as 15 people.

Since in a small parish there may be only one or two who will be anointed, the Rite of Anointing can be combined in a specific liturgy with a general healing prayer service — because we all need the healing touch and prayer of our brothers and sisters. We did this type of liturgy on Palm Sunday afternoon one year and it was a wonderful entry into Holy Week.

Don't be afraid to be creative in meeting the needs of your parish. It is important to be true to the traditions of our faith and follow the ritual requirements, but within these guidelines there is room to make these rites work effectively in your particular situation. Because of our small size, we are often able to bring a dimension to these liturgies of penance and anointing that cannot be accomplished in large parishes. We have the advantage of intimacy; let's use it to full advantage as we reconcile and heal one another.

Special Occasions

The church still maintains specific days of obligation, or holy days, although from the attendance figures in most parishes, it would be hard to tell. The *Code of Canon Law* lists Christmas, Epiphany, Ascension, the Body and Blood of Christ, Mary, Mother of God, Immaculate Conception, Assumption, St. Joseph, SS. Peter and Paul and All Saints as holy days of obligation. In the United States, discussions by our bishops have resulted in Epiphany and the Body and Blood of Christ being celebrated on Sundays and leaving the solemnities of St. Joseph and SS. Peter and Paul as holy days but not days of obligation.

That leaves the three Marian solemnities, All Saints and Ascension (although in several Western states Ascension has been moved to the Seventh Sunday of Easter). In addition, there are specific celebrations that are cultural in nature, such as the Feast of Our Lady of Guadalupe in areas with large Hispanic populations.

If there is a strong Marian devotion in your parish, it shouldn't be difficult to add a bit more festivity to the liturgy. Our pastor likes to remind us that these are not days of obligation but days of opportunity. They are additional opportunies to gather for prayer, worship and eucharist. Although this would not be an area to put a great deal of time and effort into while you are establishing a liturgical program, it can come later. Once a parish is well-grounded liturgically, these additional "opportunities" may be very welcome.

In any event, be aware that these days can enrich the life of your parish if celebrated with appropriate liturgies. Liturgies honoring your parish's patron saint, as well as other special devotions that are part of your parish's history, also provide opportunities for your community to celebrate together.

Other special occasions that arise include weddings and funerals. These require a sound knowledge of the rites and a great deal of diplomacy. Pastoral sensitivity is paramount. These are times fraught with emotion, and they can also be times that can make a real difference in people's lives. We want that difference to be positive. Bear in mind that most people's knowledge of wedding and funeral liturgies comes from memories of other weddings and funerals, and there is no need to teach them the fine points at this time.

Take weddings first. If you have enough advance notice, you have a chance to help the couple make some meaningful choices for their special day. It is very difficult to convince people that a wedding is first of all a liturgical and sacramental celebration, not a show that their friends and family will attend.

Use the Rite of Marriage to your advantage. It's vision of weddings is seldom achieved. Most couples are not aware that they have a lot of flexibility in their choice of readings and prayers; they can tailor the liturgy to be very meaningful to them. This rite offers many options and may head off some problems. Did you know that according to the rite, the entrance procession should include both the bride and the groom? Knowing this could help prevent problems with the very first thing in the liturgy — the entrance procession.

This is, however, probably one battle not worth fighting, regardless of what you may read. It simply is not part of our culture to sing a gathering song as the bridal party comes in! The "Wedding March" is so much a part of our culture that it is almost impossible to change. If both the bride and groom, and perhaps their parents, are in the procession, another piece is more appropriate anyway. I am finding that more and more couples are willing to listen to other suggestions for the procession. There are a number of good instrumental and organ processionals that can be used, such as parts of *Water Music* by Handel and the *Trumpet Voluntary in G* by Purcell. Your organist or accompanist will have other suggestions as well. But allow the bride her moment, her walk down the aisle. The people won't sing at this point anyway, since all eyes will be on the bride. A gathering song after the procession is a suggestion that works much better.

Music is always a sticking point, but this is an area where we must remain firm. No matter how much a secular song may mean to the bride and groom, it cannot be used during the Mass or nuptial liturgy. It can, however, be used as prelude music or at the reception. There are many choices for music; be prepared to help the couple make choices. But be prepared also to give them the reasoning behind the banishment of secular songs. It isn't just an arbitrary or new act: Secular music has never been approved for use in the liturgy, even though it has been used. The difference today is a growing, widening recognition of weddings as sacramental liturgies.

Have tapes of some of the music as well as their texts. Most people are not accustomed to singing at weddings, but when given the chance to participate, they do. Suggest having a cantor lead the acclamations, but don't push too hard for other singing by the assembly unless the couple is open to the idea. Another advantage in a small parish is that these people are probably already part of the parish family, and it is possible that one or more of your musicians will be available to assist with the music.

Another good wedding resource that will help couples take another look at the marriage rites is *Celebrating Marriage.*[15] Keep an eye out for other books, such as guides for the bride and groom to take home, read and discuss. These things will be helpful to them as they decide what kind of liturgy they want.

A battle over wedding music and liturgy will only lead to hard feelings and discord, so be careful of being too rigid. You may not accomplish anything but keeping Barbra Streisand's "Evergreen" out of the liturgy, but if you are sensitive to the needs and desires of those involved, you can compromise the details and not compromise the liturgy. If there are no sung acclamations, the sacrament will still be valid and the couple and parents will be more likely to leave with positive feelings about the church. This is one of the few occasions on which I am willing to bend that far, but I have listened to too many stories of wedding battles that caused life-long hard feelings toward an uncaring and unbending church. Jesus told us that the law was made for the benefit of the people, not the other way around. With the exception of secular music during the liturgy, I don't insist on anything other than that the rite be done properly.

Funeral liturgies often pose similar problems. You are dealing with people who, in their grief, may not be entirely rational. Our role as church is to comfort them, not beat them over the head with laws. The most important thing you can do is listen. People want to talk about the person they have lost. If they are not allowed to talk about it, they will not be able to move forward in the natural grief process, and they certainly won't be ready to discuss the funeral liturgy.

In a small parish, you probably will know the deceased and their family already. You will thus be in a better position to suggest lectors and readings. Many want a family member to read the scripture. Let them. This isn't a time to insist that the reader be a trained lector. You are also in a position to know what music your community knows and to help the family with these decisions. (Again, secular music is not allowed.)

Become thoroughly familiar with the new Rite of Christian Funerals. There are so many options that you can accommodate almost any need. The vigil is a wonderful opportunity to gather for a less formal liturgy with a chance to remember the life of the deceased. There is no specific provision for a rosary in the vigil service, but that doesn't mean it can't be part of it. This is a devotion that means a great deal to many people, and for them, no funeral would be complete without it.

"Funerals can begin the process of reconciling differences and supporting those ties that can help the bereaved."[16] This is a very teachable moment; people are vulnerable and open. It is an opportunity for the Holy Spirit to work in a special way.

On a personal note, it was my mother-in-law's death that brought me into the Catholic faith. I was open to hearing the call to conversion, and a very caring pastor was sensitive enough to see what was happening. This same pastor was also sensitive to the fact that most of the mourners were not Catholic, and he took time to explain the rituals so that we could understand and be part of them. It softened some life-long negative feelings toward the church held by some of my family members. Don't underestimate your role as a minister in these situations. Through the sensitivity and caring of pastors and other ministers, many have come to reconciliation after years of hurtful separation from a church perceived as uncaring.

Again, as a liturgist, become very familiar with the new Order of Christian Funerals. It is a marvelous tool. There are suggested readings, prayers and intercessions that cover every possible situation, from the person who dies a natural death from old age to the infant, from a sudden accident to a suicide. There are prayers for every age and circumstance. Being able to customize the funeral liturgy to make it very personal as well as universal is one of the greatest liturgical gifts we have been given in the new and revised rites.

The Church at Home

Especially in today's world, it is important to connect what we do on Sundays with the rest of our lives. If our liturgies fail to find a mark in everyday life, they are just Sunday decoration. We need to assist one another in living the faith we profess on Sunday — and on the job, at school or at home on Monday, Tuesday, Wednesday, Thursday, Friday and Saturday as well!

How do we bring prayer and worship back into the home? Remember that it started there long before there were parishes. As we discussed in chapter one, the church began as "house churches." During Paul's time, this was the normal place for worship. In Jewish worship a large part of prayer takes place in the home, such as the prayers that accompany meals, especially the Sabbath meal. We too need to own our faith and be responsible for its nurture in our homes and with our families. Is prayer a priority at home?

The family is a "little church" reflecting the larger church. The healthier the larger church, the healthier the little church. And it works the other way. Families who are strong in their faith at home bring a vitality to church on Sunday. Each complements the other.

For so many years, liturgy was seen as the domain of priests and religious. Lay people had their personal prayers and devotions, but liturgy meant Mass. Today, we are rediscovering our role as "little church" by using family celebrations that include scripture and prayer. During Advent we send home bulletin inserts with family prayer services for the Advent wreath, the decorating of the tree and the blessing of the crèche. There are suggestions for discussions that include all ages in preparing for Christmas.

Many parents want to do these things with their children but don't know where to begin. With this bulletin insert we not only give families a way to prepare, but because each family has the same material, there is some discussion among families. It is something to think about and talk about that has a specific focus on our Christian faith.

Another encouraging thing that is happening is a lay-organized and lay-run meeting each week to read and study the scriptures for the coming week. No, it doesn't draw large numbers, but those who do attend are growing and will affect others. This isn't something that can always be organized, but if you plant the idea, it may bear fruit. Perhaps your lectors would like to do this type of study.

If your community is not scattered geographically, another excellent lay liturgy is the Liturgy of the Hours (or Divine Office). This is morning and evening prayer built around the psalms. Priests and religious have prayed this for a very long time in the form of their "breviary" (as it is still called by many), but it is not restricted to them. Since Vatican II, the laity have been encouraged to take up this form of prayer. There are many books that contain the prayers and readings; some are more complete than others. The book my husband and I use is a four-week cycle of prayers that includes night prayer, midday prayers and the Office of Readings in addition to morning and evening prayer. It is available from most Catholic bookstores. There are many forms published, including shortened versions that include only morning and evening prayer.

I highly recommend this discipline of praying the hours. My own experience is that it keeps me connected to the larger church and helps me focus my prayer life. It has been a useful tool in our marriage, too, as a means of praying together on a regular basis. The psalms are ancient, yet they are very much in touch with today's awareness. If you are fortunate enough to live near a monastery, visit to experience the communal flow of praying this beautiful Liturgy of the Hours.

Anything you can do to foster household prayer and ritual in your parish helps to strengthen the whole parish. Use bulletin inserts and cooperate with your religious education program. Recommend books like *Catholic Household Blessings and Prayers,* from the National Conference of Catholic Bishops, and the *Book of Blessings,* from the Vatican Congregation for Divine Worship. Both contain a variety of prayers and blessings for use in almost any circumstance on almost any occasion.

Our people need to understand that ritual and prayer are not restricted to the clergy or to the church building. Prayer is at the heart of the renewal of both the church and the liturgy. In the foreword to *Household Blessings and Prayers,* the Bishops' Committee says, "Prayer must happen in the 'little churches' — the households, the families — if the Sunday assembly is to become a community of prayer." The daily prayers of our people, joined to our prayers in the Sunday assembly, help us to know who we are as church — the Body of Christ.

●

1 Hayyim Schauss, Guide to Jewish Holy Days *(Union of Hebrew Congregations, 1938).*

2 My own realization of the real significance of this celebration was born from Gabe Huck's introduction to Mary Ann Simcoe, ed., Parish Path Through Lent and Eastertime *(Chicago: Liturgy Training Publications, 1985). He points out that our whole church year culminates with the Easter Vigil, a celebration of such magnitude that the "Vigil can be only within the Triduum, and that can be only when there is a Lent and Eastertime."*

3 General Norms for the Liturgical Year and Calendar, #*27.*

4 Marty Haugen, "Mass of Remembrance" (Chicago: GIA Publications, 1987).

5 David Haas, "Song of the Body of Christ" (Chicago: GIA Publications, 1989).

6 Christopher Walker, "My God, My God" (Portland: Oregon Catholic Press, 1989).

7 General Norms for the Liturgical Year and the Calendar, #*18.*

8 William J. Freburger, This is the Word of the Lord *(Notre Dame, IN: Ave Maria Press, 1984).*

9 See note 8, chaper 4.

10 General Norms for the Liturgical Year and the Calendar, #*39.*

11 The Rites, *vol. 1 and 2 [The Roman Rite revised by Decree of the Second Vatican Council] (Collegeville, MN: Pueblo Publishing Co., 1990).*

12 Oliver Crilly, ed., Penitential Services *(Dublin, Ireland: The Columbia Press, 1986).*

13 "Pastoral Care of the Sick," The Rites, *chapter 4, section 99. See note 11, chapter 8.*

14 Andrew J. Witchger, The Rite of Anointing *(St. Louis, MO: Morning Star Publishers, 1991).*

15 Paul Covino, ed., Celebrating Marriage *(Washington, DC: The Pastoral Press, 1994).*

16 Order of Christian Funerals, #*13, as in* The Rites *(see note 11, chapter 8).*

CHAPTER 9

We Are a Pilgrim People

Conversion and Journey

The word conversion comes from the Latin prefix *con,* which means "together," and the verb *vertere,* which means "to transform or turn around." Transform in turn comes from the Latin prefix *trans,* meaning across, beyond or through, so as to change, and *formare,* meaning to form. So literally, when we speak of conversion we speak of turning around or of going beyond, across or through something in order to change together. Though initiation itself takes place only once, conversion is not at all a one-time occurrence.

It is important to recognize that conversion isn't something that happens just when a non-Catholic "converts" and becomes Catholic. It is an ongoing process. We are a work in progress. What we are now is known, but what we shall become is not quite clear. Pope John Paul II says we are a pilgrim people, living in the tension of the already but not yet. The reign of God is at hand, but we aren't there yet.

This journey, this ongoing conversion process in our lives, is facilitated by strong community ties with others on the same journey. This is why our parish life is so important. Having others around us who share our struggle to live gospel lives helps us when that path gets rocky. Raising our children with others who share our values makes it easier to pass on our faith.

As we grow as a parish, the conversion process is evident in our communal lives as well. When we, as a community, see ourselves as responsible for bringing the love of God to the world around us in our deeds and words, we look for ways to reach out to others. We can, as a community and as individuals, make a difference in our world.

Although we may lack numbers, that does not prevent us from having a great effect on the world around us. Remember that originally, Jesus had only a handful of followers; yet the difference they made is why we are who we are. The 80 families at my parish, St. Anne's in the Mountains, have made a big difference for many people in our community. Through our community, we feed between 65 and 100 families every month. There is a great deal of poverty in our area, much of it hidden. By pooling individual resources, both of time and money, we are able to be part of a food program that purchases food in bulk at substantial savings. Through this effort, there are children in our area who don't go to bed hungry at night.

Why do these people give so generously of their time and money? Because they have come to understand on a personal level what living a gospel life means. There has been a conversion in their lives. Has liturgy played a part in this? I hope so. By gathering for worship as a community, we have heard the word, the call to serve God by serving others, and have found the strength as a people to go and live what we have heard.

Infant Baptism

This process of conversion is of great importance in our church as well. Outside of liturgical changes, none of the changes since Vatican II have affected the face of our church more than the change in our process of initiating new members, both infants and adults.

We have come to realize that this process involves all of us. It is no longer a private affair. We used to bring newborns to church on a Sunday afternoon for a minimal rite, often before their mothers were able to attend. The understanding of baptism as an entry into the Body of Christ was not well understood. Rather, it was an obligation, almost a superstition, to baptize as quickly as possible in order to protect the child from going to limbo if he or she died.

For something that was never official church doctrine, limbo was, and in some places still is, a widely held belief. In preparing families who are seeking baptism for their babies, you will still encounter the belief that all unbaptized babies who die go to limbo. A loving explanation of the nature of baptism and of God's love can help in this situation, but it may also require a conversation with the pastor. Don't let it become a point of contention or make you lose sight of the intention of the parents to raise their child in the faith.

There are times when baptism may be denied, and these are difficult situations. This is a pastoral decision made by the pastor, not by a lay person, but you need to have a good understanding of why and when this is done. For example, "An infant should be baptized within the first weeks after birth. In the complete absence of any well-founded hope that the infant will be brought up in the Catholic religion, the baptism is to be delayed, in conformity with the provision of particular law (see no. 25), and the parents are to be informed of the reasons."[1] In this case, baptism is not permanently denied but is delayed until there is the reasonable expectation that the child will be raised in the faith.

That expectation may come from grandparents, active godparents or other relatives who are active Catholics and are active in the life of the child. It also may come from a renewal of faith on the part of one or both parents. This can be a major event in the conversion process of the parents. It is a difficult situation, but we keep faith that God is working in the lives of everyone involved for the good of everyone involved.

We understand that baptism brings the baby into the mystical Body of Christ and is the first step of the initiation process. We also realize that infant baptism requires the responsibility of passing along our faith, of helping this child come to know God and Jesus in community and to live as a Christian. We also are beginning to understand that it is the responsibility of the community to help make this possible. Baptism is the first of many steps along the pilgrim path to God.

This change to a communal emphasis works very well in a small parish. We are able to use the entire rite, from the entry into the church at the beginning of Mass to the sacrament itself after the homily. The entire community is there to witness the occasion and to be reminded of its obligations to that child and to his or her family. It can be a very meaningful experience for everyone concerned.

In preparing for a liturgy at which a baptism is to be celebrated, communicate that fact to everyone involved, especially the musicians. It is rare that the readings of the day will support the sacrament directly, but often the music selected can help bridge the gap. A sung Alleluia to welcome the new member is a natural touch.[2]

We must be sure to take our part, sharing our faith by being present for both child and family during the formative years. The initiation rites will continue with the child's first communion at about age seven, and the rites of confirmation at whatever age is the current norm in your diocese.

The RCIA

One of the most far-reaching changes made by Vatican II was the reinstitution of the catechumenate as the norm for receiving new adult members into the church. It is still evolving, as experience reveals hidden weaknesses and strengths in the process. The Rite of Christian Initiation of Adults has changed not only the way we receive new members but also the face of our liturgies and our parishes.

In earlier years, a person seeking either baptism or full communion with the Catholic faith was instructed individually by a priest. The actual baptism or profession of faith was usually done in private also. This was in keeping with the generally privatized and individual nature of worship itself prior to Vatican II. Part of the radical change after Vatican II was a change in the way we looked at liturgy and worship. They were to become cooperative and assembly oriented, with the full and active participation mandated in the *Constitution on the Sacred Liturgy.* As parishes, we became communities rather than groups of individuals.

The new rite makes clear that the job of initiating new members belongs to the community as a whole. This has meant becoming welcoming communities willing to share our faith with those seeking to join us. In the process, many "cradle Catholics" are relearning what it means to be Catholic. If this faith of ours is so important that others are willing to spend months seeking admission, we may want to look again to see what it is that we have taken for granted.

In a large parish this process can become so large that it takes on an existence of its own; it is almost a community within a community. It has transformed many parishes by adding new vitality and vibrance to their liturgies and to their community. In a small parish, the process must adapt to meet a different set of needs. But the initiation of new members enriches the small parish too, as long as it is done with attention to the spirit of the process and the rites.

As a liturgist, your first step is to read and understand the rites and rituals and the processes that go with them. Liturgy Training Publications publishes a study edition of *The Rite of Christian Initiation of Adults* that includes the complete text of the rites used during each stage of the catechumenate. *The Rites* also gives the full rites as well as information about their development and proper usage. It is important to have a good overview of the process, the rites and all the variations available.

There are four major steps in the journey to initiation: (1) Upon reaching the point of initial conversion and wishing to become a Christian, the inquirer is accepted as a catechumen; (2) the catechumen is accepted into a more intense period of preparation for the sacraments of initiation; and (3) the catechumen receives the sacraments of initiation. Each of these steps is marked by a liturgical rite that follows a period of inquiry and growth. Then, (4) the neophyte experiences a period of mystagogia, or postbaptismal catechesis. These rites are important not only to the one seeking initiation but also to the community as a whole.

The first step is a period of inquiry, a time of sharing faith journeys with others in the community. It is a time of evangelization and discernment. The community's role is that of setting examples and welcoming. At the end of this time, however long it may be, is the rite of acceptance into the Order of the Catechumens. By the time an inquirer has reached this point in a small community, that person should be pretty well known to the community.

Because there may be, and often is, only one person taking part in the process in a small parish, this initial rite of acceptance can be held whenever the time is right. Because there are not large numbers, we can be more flexible in our initiation process. Larger parishes have set times, usually during Advent. The rite calls for waiting until there are sufficient numbers to form a group for the next step (*The Rites,* 18). That's fine in a larger parish, but if we were to wait, the inquirer might wait two or three years! Adapt the schedule to fit the needs of your parish.

Now begins the process of learning the faith. This does not mean Catholic Doctrine 101 but rather a sharing through the word of God of what it means to be a Christian, specifically, a Catholic Christian. Here again, the examples of the community as a whole and of the specific individuals working with the catechumen play a major role. In our parish, we have teamed up with another nearby parish for the preparation of both catechumens and candidates (those already baptized who are asking to become Catholic). Our deacon and his wife work with them and their sponsors, and call upon various members of the community to share their lives and experiences from time to time.

There is no set time limit for this process. The tendency has been to run the RCIA program on almost a school year schedule, with acceptance into the catechumenate on the First Sunday of Advent, the rite of election on the First Sunday of Lent and initiation at the Easter Vigil. The only fixed date should be the Vigil. Some people are ready sooner, others later. Here again, the small parish can adapt to the individual rather than making the individual adapt to the group.

During this period of catechesis, there are numerous minor rites that can be celebrated which help give the catechumen a sense of liturgy. The rites also call for the catechumen to be dismissed during the Mass, after the homily, to go with a catechist to study the day's scripture. Those remaining at Mass begin to understand more clearly the significance of their own baptismal status. In reality, most small parishes simply don't have the resources to do this. The exception is during the next stage of the process, during which a dismissal is necessary.

When the catechumen is ready to proceed, there is a rite of election that comes at the beginning of Lent. This is followed by a more intense period of preparation for the sacraments, the period of purification and enlightenment, and includes the celebration of specific rites. The most visible of these rites are the scrutinies, which are part of Mass on the third, fourth and fifth Sundays of Lent. It is important to have a good understanding of these rites when you are planning your Lenten liturgies. It is a time of importance and catechesis for the whole community.

There are specific pieces of music that can accompany many of the rituals during the whole process. If these become part of the assembly's repertoire, they are available as needed. Most pew resources have a section on RCIA outlining the rites and suggesting music. Don't be afraid to find other music that fits the occasion if it is better suited for your parish.

On those Sundays when the scrutinies are celebrated, we also proclaim the Cycle A readings regardless of which cycle is current. It is important to inform your lectors of this so that they prepare the correct readings. If you have additional Masses, you can use either Cycle A or the current cycle.

During this Lenten period, the dismissal is an important and visual element of the process. Try to have someone available to work with the elect for these Sundays. The candidates, who are already baptized, do not need to be dismissed. They may choose to leave at that point, but if there are no elect, there are no scrutinies and no dismissals.

One point here: If you are working with a combined group of baptized candidates and unbaptized elect, be sure to differentiate them. You don't want to make it appear that the baptized status of the candidates is not important. Part of the Creed says that we believe in "one baptism for the forgiveness of sin." These people are already members of the mystical Body of Christ. They are seeking full communion in the Roman Catholic faith. This needs to be made clear, not just at this point but throughout the process, in both word and ritual.

The rites of initiation at the Easter Vigil will require your liturgical skills in cooperation with the coordinator of the RCIA program and the pastor. And in the case of small parishes, these rites may have to be adapted on a yearly basis to adjust to the current situation. One year you may have no candidates and no elect, or perhaps an infant baptism. Another year you may have one or the other or both. Our parish recently had two candidates for reception by profession and a child to be baptized. Before that, we had one adult baptized and one received by profession. This is why knowledge of the rituals and rites is necessary: You must be able to put together a smooth liturgy, written out clearly and completely. You want the assembly to be drawn into the rite rather than being distracted by the celebrant or deacon trying to find his place.

During the time between Easter and Pentecost, the period of mystagogy is celebrated. As we said earlier, this is a time of postbaptismal catechesis. It is also a time for both the neophyte (the new member) and the community to deepen their understanding of the paschal mystery. In this period, the neophyte will fully experience the sacraments that have been studied and anticipated.

Don't forget the children in this process. The new rites of initiation also include children who have reached the age of reason, usually about seven (RCIC). These children are to receive the same training, in a process similar to that of the adults but adapted for their age. They are to receive the complete initiation rites also — baptism, confirmation and first communion.

As with most other "rules," pastoral flexibility is necessary here. For children, part of the value of this process is the faith journey with other children. If there are no other children, some type of one-on-one program will be needed. If the child is part of a family coming into the church, it is important to prepare all of them at the appropriate level so that their initiation at the Easter Vigil is a family affair.

The return of the catechumenate is one of the greatest gifts of Vatican II. It takes more work. It takes more organization. It takes more time. But when done well, the faith life of the entire parish is enriched. It opens a community to the riches of their faith, explored on an adult level, and it results in the conversion of not only the catechumens but others as well. The new members revive our enthusiasm and help us regain a sense of awe at the wonderful love and mercy of our God.

●

1 "Introduction to the Rite of Baptism," 8.3, as in The Rites. See note 11, chapter 8.

2 For more on the liturgy of infant baptism, see Timothy Fitzgerald, Infant Baptism: A Parish Celebration (Chicago: Liturgy Training Publications, 1994).

CHAPTER 10

More about Education

Basic Education

The first chapter discussed the importance of basic education in liturgy. In the ensuing chapters, you have seen the importance of learning and knowing the rites that make up our liturgy. In small parishes we must adapt to fit the circumstances. To do this, we need to understand both the letter of the law and the spirit of the law. Yes, these liturgical documents are liturgical canon law; the actual *Code of Canon Law* contains relatively little by way of liturgical guidelines but rather refers to the sacred books as the source of liturgical law.

The sacramentary, lectionary, *Ceremonial of Bishops,* rite books and other liturgy documents outline the rituals themselves and, in their introductions, give history, rationale and other pertinent information. These constitute the authority for our liturgical practices. It sounds like a lot of reading, and it is. But once you get started, the material will hold your attention if you have an interest in liturgy. Since you have read this far in this book, I will assume you have that interest.

Some of this reading is very detailed, and you will go back to it frequently, each time seeing something you missed before. While I was writing this book, there were whole sections I had forgotten about or perhaps saw differently than the last time I'd read them. But this is what is exciting about education, regardless of the field. There is always something new to learn.

Some of the purposes and material in various documents has been referenced in earlier chapters. What follows is a complete listing of these documents. It gives a quick overview of each of them and how they relate to each other and to the liturgy in general.

So where do you begin in this quest for knowledge? In the first chapter, I referred to the *Constitution on the Sacred Liturgy* (CSL) of Vatican II. This document is the basic foundation, revealing the history, doctrine and perspectives that were the basis for all the other liturgical documents promulgated since that time. The changes in and the development of the post–Vatican II liturgical books, such as our sacramentary and lectionary, are outlined here. It also explains the reasoning behind and implementation of such changes as using the vernacular, receiving communion in the hand and receiving communion under the form of both bread and wine.

The next most important document is the *General Instruction of the Roman Missal,* (GIRM) which sets forth the doctrines and norms for eucharistic celebration and other forms of liturgy. It can be found in the beginning of the sacramentary as well as in *The Liturgy Documents.* These instructions and the sacramentary are prerequisite reading to understanding the flow of liturgy. Everything is there — every word, every gesture, every detail. The correct vestments and seasonal colors are given. The directions for processions and special rituals are there. It's a basic how-to-say-Mass manual! No one can remember every detail, especially for those celebrations that occur only once a year or occasionally. But it is all here for review when needed. Reading the GIRM thoroughly and becoming familiar with its pattern and flow is a very enlightening and enriching experience. But it is, to continue our original analogy, only part of the foundation.

Knowledge of the structure and rubrics (the directions printed in red ink) is important, but without an understanding of the history and theology that lie behind those words, liturgical planning tends to be very rigid and legalistic. This is a common problem with all of us in the beginning stages of our liturgical formation. Rather than giving an explanation, we can only answer the question of why we are doing something with "because the book says so." For every symbol and every ritual, for every prayer and every particular action, there is a reason, a history, a theology, a meaning that needs to be understood. Becoming aware of these opens up the liturgies so that they can be not only well done but pastorally done for the growth and understanding of our particular parish.

In addition to the GIRM, it is important to read the *Appendix to the General Instructions of the Dioceses in the U.S.* (GIAPP), also found in *The Liturgy Documents.* It contains specific adaptations that were made by the National Conference of Catholic Bishops (NCCB) pertinent to our local celebrations. For example, GIRM #66 refers to readers or lectors only as "he," indicating that this ministry is filled by men only. The Appendix specifically provides for women in this ministry as well as in the ministries of cantor, commentator, song leader, and so on. So the two documents need to be read together.

Once the sacramentary and the GIRM are studied, one needs to move on to the *Lectionary for Mass: Introduction* (LMIN). Again, the entire lectionary is a very educational resource, and the liturgist must be familiar with its entire contents. It doesn't need to be memorized, but you need to be familiar enough with this document to locate needed references. It provides many little-known but useful facts. For example, it highlights the fact that our Catholic liturgy is thoroughly biblical. As one commentator has said, "Any Catholic congregation where the Mass is not recognizable as (a Bible service) has not given sufficient attention to what the *Introduction* has to say."[1]

A thorough study of LMIN will also furnish insight into the structure of the lectionary, how the readings relate to one another and to the season and how texts were selected. There are guidelines for various options and explanations of the seasonal cycles of readings. All in all, it provides a very good understanding of not just the importance of the readings but also the nature of the word of God as expressed in both the liturgy of the word and the liturgy of the eucharist.

The other documents of primary importance are *Music in Catholic Worship* (MCW), *Environment and Art in Catholic Worship* (EACW) and *Liturgical Music Today* (LMT), which updated MCW. These documents present a better understanding of the totality of liturgy, the fact that all elements flow together not like beads on a string but like a seamless garment with an unbroken line. They put to rest the idea that either music or the environment of the worship space are optional luxuries. These areas are, in fact, integral parts of the liturgy and must be approached as such.

General Norms for the Liturgical Year (GNLY) supplies the theology of and guidelines for our liturgical year and its cycle of seasons, feasts and solemnities. This document presents the liturgical calendar, the basic schedule of our liturgies each year. It emphasizes the paschal mystery as the center of all our celebrations and gives us not only the cycle of seasons but the order of priority for the various feasts, solemnities and memorials.

An additional resource necessary for understanding and preparing specific liturgies better is *The Rites,* volumes one and two. Building on the doctrines and liturgical laws of the documents and sacred books, it outlines specific rituals. *The Rites* contains all the sacramental liturgies other than the usual eucharistic celebration. The complete order of worship, with rubrics, is given for the various forms of baptism (adult, infant, within Mass or outside of Mass), the various forms of marriage (with or without Mass and mixed marriages), all the rites for the Rite of Christian Initiation of Adults and various types of funerals. (More specific rites and many resources for funerals may also be found in the Rites of Christian Burial.)

Beyond this essential reading, there are additional documents and books that assist in broadening one's base of knowledge. The remaining liturgical documents are necessary for a more complete understanding of liturgy. In particular, *This Holy and Living Sacrifice: A Directory for the Celebration and Reception of Communion Under Both Kinds* (HLS) is necessary for a fuller understanding of this change in holy communion to reception of both the body and the blood of the Lord. It is, like the Appendix to GIRM, a document by the NCCB containing diocesan policies normative to the United States.

In order to gain a better perspective on the traditions and rites, a study of church history is essential. Who we are and how we reached this point in our history is not only interesting, it helps us understand why we as the Roman Catholic church exist in our present form today.[2]

Along the same historical lines but focused in a more concentrated way on the liturgy is Edward Foley's *From Age to Age.*[3] This book is an in-depth study that traces the development of our Christian eucharistic celebrations from our earliest Jewish roots to the present time. Foley uses architecture, music, books and vessels to explain the history and development of our current celebrations. It certainly puts to rest the old excuse we always hear against doing anything different: "We've *always* done it like this!"

There are volumes of detailed studies of the eucharist, ranging from its history to current liturgical practices. Still others detail the eucharistic prayer, its development and its significance, and suggest ways for improving this important ritual in our liturgies.

There are many other very instructive books, too numerous to mention, that will help satisfy your thirst for knowledge. For a person without a firm grounding in liturgical principles and doctrine, however, there is no way to know if they are theologically or pastorally sound, or up-to-date. So use good judgment and ground yourself in the principles first.

Continuing Education

Recognizing the importance of an educated laity involved in ministry, many dioceses offer courses in such areas as basic theology, leadership skills, pastoral ministry and liturgical formation. For many years there have been certificate programs for religious education teachers and catechists. Now there are more and more certificate programs for other areas of ministry. If you are in one of these dioceses, it would be in your best interest to take advantage of the opportunity. In some cases, diocesan programs are conducted in conjunction with a Catholic college or university in the area.

If you have the time, desire and opportunity, many of these schools now offer programs in pastoral and liturgical formation. Their offerings range from certificate programs to graduate degrees. For the most part, however, liturgists with degrees are found in larger parishes and are salaried professionals. Smaller parishes, of which we speak here, must rely on "homegrown" volunteers. That doesn't mean our education is less important or our abilities less but that we get much of our education from experience and less from formal training. It also usually means that our payment is in the satisfaction gained from liturgies well done. But it doesn't mean we can't or don't avail ourselves of opportunities for higher education.

It is also a good idea to start your own liturgical library. Because I do most of my work at home, I find that having the basics at my fingertips is most helpful. *The Liturgy Documents,* a small sacramentary and a small lectionary are a good place to start. These are available through most Catholic bookstores and are not expensive. The other resource I use frequently is *The Rites,* volumes one and two. After that, you will find that whenever the opportunity arises, you will expand your library according to your needs and interests.

Education is a marvelous experience. Each time you learn something new, it impacts what you already know, leading to deeper insights and more questions to which you seek answers — leading to even more questions! It's a wonderfully exciting cycle. The more we know, the more we know how much we don't know.

You Are Not Alone

You don't have to struggle by yourself for training and assistance; there are programs available in most dioceses. In talking to various dioceses around the country, I've observed that a pattern develops. Most offer at least annual diocesan training programs in liturgy, either as a whole or for specific ministries, and most hold a major liturgy conference or at least have access to one.

For example, the archdiocese of Los Angeles hosts both a large religious education congress, with workshops in liturgical areas as well, and a liturgical convention each year. The regional Southwest liturgical conference is held annually in different states. It covers Texas, Oklahoma, New Mexico, Colorado, Wyoming and Utah. Vermont holds both a religious education congress with liturgical workshops and a faith festival that is focused more directly on liturgy.

The archdiocese of Omaha, Nebraska, has 105 rural parishes scattered over a large area. Their program for training eucharistic ministers at the diocesan level consists of holding four-hour sessions in various locations each fall. At the end of the training sessions, everyone comes to a commissioning ceremony and receives their mandate from the archbishop. They also make training in other ministries available when requested.

Wyoming has primarily medium-sized to small parishes scattered over the entire state. They do offer diocesan training programs in liturgy, but they also have a large video library available to their most remote parishes.

Though I didn't contact every diocese, I did talk to people involved in liturgy training from several dioceses representing a fairly good cross-section of the country, and I primarily focused on those with a large number of small and/or rural parishes. There seems to be a definite awareness of the need for liturgical training and a growing interest on the part of the laity in receiving that training.

The frequent comment made by dioceses was that although the training is available, if the pastor isn't supportive, the training resources aren't used. It was interesting that the priests I spoke with also commented that resistance from their fellow priests hinders liturgical development. This is a problem that only prayer and patience will solve.

It was also interesting to note that most of the priests felt that their laity wanted to be involved and to take part in the ownership of their parishes and liturgies. When liturgy is done well, the parish draws more people. But in most smaller parishes, there is rarely a liturgist. There may be someone who schedules lectors or ministers or someone who oversees a music program, but there is no overall director. When there is such an individual, that person is a volunteer who takes his or her education upon themselves, sometimes with monetary support and sometimes without.

So it is apparent that improving the liturgy is important to large numbers of people and that educational opportunities are available. What is required of the potential liturgist is to seek out whatever training is available. One suggestion is a type of mentoring program between large parishes and small ones. It could be a sister parish arrangement, in which those who have the training and education assist those who need it but don't have the resources to obtain it.

Already a large percentage of small parishes are having to share a pastor. So the quality of their liturgical life will become more and more the responsibility of the laity. By continuing to educate ourselves and by working in cooperation with each other and our pastors, there is much to look forward to in our future liturgies.

●

1 Gerard S. Sloyan, "Overview to the Lectionary for Mass: Introduction," in The Liturgy Documents: A Parish Resource *(Chicago: Liturgy Training Publications, 1991), 119.*

2 A good source for this that is easy to read and comprehend is William J. Bausch, Pilgrim Church *(Mystic, CT: Twenty-third Publications, 1981).*

3 Edward Foley, From Age to Age: How Christians Have Celebrated the Eucharist *(Chicago: Liturgy Training Publications, 1991).*

Conclusion

Hopefully this book has opened your eyes to the many possibilities that can add to the richness of our liturgies. We need to recapture the sense of mystery and awe that seems to be lacking, or at least diminished, in today's celebrations. That is one of the complaints I often hear when people reminisce about the old Latin Mass. They felt a sense of mystery then. That mystery is still there — I think we sometimes just talk it to death!

The emphasis often seems to be on how quickly we can "get through with Mass" rather on how well we celebrate. In large parishes that have five or six Masses every Sunday with 30 minutes between them, as well as parking lot problems, this is more understandable. However, it is still a sad commentary on our priorities. In our small parishes, there are not such constraints.

Good liturgy takes as long as it takes to celebrate well. However, I don't find that it takes any more time to celebrate well. By respecting the natural silences that are built into the rituals and by doing those rituals properly, we can bring that mystery and awe back to Mass. It needs to be a spiritual oasis where we can come to lay the everyday world aside for a time and be nourished, strengthened and encouraged. Then we can reenter that other world "in peace, to love and serve the Lord."

For that other world is where our Lord has commanded us to go, bringing good news to the poor, comfort for the afflicted and justice for the oppressed. It is very easy to become so wrapped up in liturgy that it becomes the end rather than the means to an end. The liturgy itself becomes an idol, something to be done for its own sake rather than for God and the kingdom.

I had the opportunity not long ago to hear a presentation by Father Gregory J. Boyle, a Jesuit priest who is the director of a program called Jobs for a Future. He works in downtown Los Angeles at Dolores Mission with gang members and "at risk" youth. He opened my eyes on several levels. For many people in that area, their faith is what keeps them going. It is a glimmer of hope in an otherwise hopeless world. Liturgy is a source of strength for them.

With all the headlines about gang warfare and drive-by shootings, it is very easy to dismiss these young people as worthless. But they are also children of God and need our help, our hope and our prayers. Listening to Father Boyle talk about these kids, we heard about their fears and their dreams. We heard about the fears of a young boy who had two children. He wanted so much to be a good father, but he didn't know how. He'd never had an example. And he knew he could end up dead at any time. Father Boyle reminded us of the humanity of this young boy and his friends.

What does this have to do with liturgy? Saint James tells us that faith apart from works is dead (2:26). Saint Paul says that faith without love amounts to nothing (1 Corinthians 13:2). Jesus told us to love one another, and the gospels spend a great deal of time telling us what that means — feeding the poor, clothing the naked, visiting the prisoner and all the other works of mercy and charity. Our faith calls us to live gospel lives, and our faith is nourished by our liturgies — or at least it should be.

We are all called to a specific task in this world. Some are called to run soup kitchens, others to run missions in inner cities or foreign cities and others to help gang members find jobs. Some are called to provide music, proclaim scripture and help us understand our history and theology. And some are called to help provide our worship experiences.

At a retreat on social justice, another Jesuit priest, Father Max Oliva, pointed out that not everyone is called to be on the front lines in the fight for social justice but that all of us are called to support these works with prayer. Our liturgies must provide not only that type of guidance but the opportunity to act upon it. They must be there as a place for workers to be renewed and supported.

In the everyday world, we don't live in church. Most of us have families to tend, jobs to do and all the other tasks associated with life. In a world that increasingly rejects moral standards and calls us to a life of personal pleasure, it is difficult to live by Christ's standards. Where can we go to be strengthened in our resolve and be supported by others involved in the same struggle? Hopefully, to our parish family.

So the ministry of liturgist has a far wider reach. Celebrating liturgy helps put things in perspective and calls each of us to be attentive to what is really important. It is where we can be nourished and sustained by the word and fed by the gift of Christ's body in the eucharist and in each other.

As you grow in this ministry, my hope is that you will come to love the treasure that is ours in the rites and symbols of this Catholic faith and pass that love on to others. May the power of those rituals, through the grace of God, enable us all to love, praise and serve the Lord, and love and serve one another. God bless you.

●

Added Assistance

Even with the best intentions and lots of energy, a liturgist can be left not knowing where to turn. There are many helpful resources from which you can choose. Below is a list of several places that have been helpful to me in my work. Perhaps they might be of assistance to you, too. Most will be glad to send their catalogs.

Liturgy Training Publications
1800 N. Hermitage Ave.
Chicago IL 60622-1101
1-800-933-1800

Alverno Religious Art & Books
5243-53 W. Irving Park Rd.
Chicago IL 60641
1-800-333-3446

Catholic Book Publishing Company
257 W. 17th St.
New York NY 10011

C.M. Almy & Sons
10 Glenville St., Box 2628
Greenwich CT 06836
1-800-225-2569

GIA Publications
7404 S. Mason Ave.
Chicago IL 60638
1-708-496-3800

The Liturgical Conference
8750 Georgia Ave.
Silver Spring MD 20910-3621

The Liturgical Press
P.O. Box 7500
Collegeville MN 56321-7500
1-800-858-5450

Meyer-Vogelpohl
717 Race St.
Cincinnati OH 45202
1-800-543-0264

Oregon Catholic Press
5536 NE Hassalo
Portland OR 97213
1-800-LITURGY (548-8749)

Pastoral Press (part of National Association of Pastoral Musicians)
225 Sheridan St. NW
Washington DC 20011-1492

Paulist Press
997 Macarthur Blvd.
Mahwah NJ 07430

United States Catholic Conference
3211 Fourth St. NE
Washington DC 20017-1194
1-800-235-8722

World Library Publications
3815 N. Willow Rd.
Schiller Park IL 60176
1-800-621-5197